DESIGN
IN THE AGE OF
DARWIN

D1452036

MARY AND LEIGH BLOCK MUSEUM OF ART
Northwestern University

NORTHWESTERN UNIVERSITY PRESS

STEPHEN F. EISENMAN

with Corinne Granof

DESIGN
IN THE AGE OF
DARWIN

FROM
WILLIAM MORRIS
TO FRANK LLOYD WRIGHT

Published in conjunction with the exhibition *Design in the Age of Darwin: From William Morris to Frank Lloyd Wright*, Mary and Leigh Block Museum of Art, Northwestern University, May 9–August 24, 2008

Design in the Age of Darwin has been generously funded by the Terra Foundation for American Art; the Myers Foundations; the Alice Kaplan Center for the Humanities; the Graduate School, Northwestern University; the Alumnae of Northwestern University; Illinois Arts Council, a state agency; American Airlines; the Graham Foundation for Advanced Studies in the Fine Arts; Elizabeth F. Cheney Foundation; John Notz, Jr.; and Arete Swartz Warren.

The Paul Mellon Centre for Studies in British Art has supported the publication of this exhibition catalogue.

Published by the Mary and Leigh Block Museum of Art, Northwestern University and Northwestern University Press, Evanston, Illinois 60208

Design and production by Diane Jaroch Design
Copyedited by Northwestern University Relations
Printed in China by Oceanic Graphic Printing Co.

Library of Congress Cataloging-in-Publication Data

Eisenman, Stephen.
Design in the age of Darwin: from William Morris to Frank Lloyd Wright/ By Stephen F. Eisenman, with Corinne Granof.
p. cm.
Includes bibliographical references and index.

"Design in the Age of Darwin: From William Morris to Frank Lloyd Wright is published in conjunction with an exhibition organized by the Mary and Leigh Block Museum of Art, Northwestern University ... May 9–August 24, 2008."

ISBN-13: 978-0-8101-5204-5
(pbk. : alk. paper)
ISBN-10: 0-8101-5204-5
(pbk. : alk. paper)

1. Darwin, Charles, 1809–1882--Influence--Exhibitions. 2. Art and design--History--19th century--Exhibitions. 3. Art and design--History--20th century--Exhibitions. 4. Decoration and ornament--History--19th century--Exhibitions. 5. Decoration and ornament--History--20th century--Exhibitions. 6. Modernism (Aesthetics)--Great Britain--History--19th century--Exhibitions. 7. Modernism (Aesthetics)--Great Britain--History--20th century--Exhibitions. 8. Modernism (Aesthetics)--United States--History--19th century--Exhibitions. 9. Modernism (Aesthetics)--United States--History--20th century--Exhibitions. I. Granof, Corinne. II. Mary and Leigh Block Museum of Art. III. Title.

NK1370.E37 2008
745.409034--dc22

2008010222

Contents

As the fine arts museum of Northwestern University, the Mary and Leigh Block Museum of Art contributes to the University's teaching and scholarship by organizing original, thought-provoking exhibitions, often engaging faculty and students in the curatorial process. One of our goals in this is to serve as a national leader among university museums in taking new critical and creative approaches to multidisciplinary learning through the visual arts—an endeavor exemplified, as its title suggests, in the exhibition *Design in the Age of Darwin: From William Morris to Frank Lloyd Wright*.

One of the greatest minds of the 19th century, British scientist Charles Darwin challenged the foundations of Western culture with his revolutionary theories on the origins of life. That his ideas provoked strong reactions from the scientific community and biblical literalists of his day—and that they still have the power to stir controversy—is well known. Explored in the pages that follow are the less well-known aspects of Darwin's direct and indirect influences on the visual and decorative arts. The exhibition thesis, developed by curator and professor Stephen Eisenman, finds its inspiration in the artistic output as well as the writings of many artists and designers working in the late 19th and early 20th centuries. Darwin's pervasive influence can be found on both sides of the Atlantic, from the international Arts and Crafts movement to the Prairie School.

The Block Museum's presentation of the exhibition corresponds with many celebrations including the initiative by the Terra Foundation for American Art, *American Art American City*, taking place throughout Chicago in 2008; as well as the 200th anniversary commemorations of the birth of Charles Darwin; and the 150th anniversary of the publication of his seminal work *On the Origin of Species* in 2009.

This Block-organized exhibition and related publication would not have been possible without the dedication of Stephen F. Eisenman who brought a wealth of knowledge and expertise to conceive of the project. Professor Eisenman worked closely with Block Museum curator Corinne Granof, who helped realize the project through the practical coordination of the exhibition and publication. I share with Dr. Granof in thanking everyone who so generously helped bring this project to fruition.

DAVID ALAN ROBERTSON
The Ellen Philips Katz Director

Acknowledgments

Design in the Age of Darwin: From William Morris to Frank Lloyd Wright traces how a scientific principle debated in academic and public fields influenced designers and architects and was apparent in decorative forms in England and the United States in the late 19th and early 20th centuries. The community of a university is the ideal setting to realize this exhibition and publication. Guest curator Stephen F. Eisenman has brought extraordinary insight and connections to the materials. In putting together the book and exhibition, Stephen Eisenman worked with Northwestern University Professor David Van Zanten, who has contributed an essay on the designs of Louis Sullivan, along with graduate students Angelina Lucento, Jacob Lewis, and Zirwat Chowdhury. The graduate students in Professor Eisenman's Darwin seminar and undergraduates in his Museum Studies course all contributed to the evolution of the exhibition and this publication. Undergraduate Elliot Reichert has been exceptionally helpful. Edna Togba, who served as the Graduate Fellow at the Block Museum this academic year, gave this project careful attention and provided perseverance and patience in gathering and organizing information.

We are grateful to the supporters of this project, which include the Myers Foundations; the Alice Kaplan Center for the Humanities; the Graduate School, Northwestern University; the Alumnae of Northwestern University; Illinois Arts Council, a state agency; American Airlines; the Graham Foundation for Advanced Studies in the Fine Arts; Elizabeth F. Cheney Foundation; the Terra Foundation for American Art; John Notz, Jr.; and Arete Swartz Warren. The Paul Mellon Centre for Studies in British Art has generously supported the publication of this exhibition catalogue.

All the generous lenders to the exhibition made it possible to display and rediscover objects of decorative design and to consider them in ways that appreciate not only their aesthetic value, but to understand them as manifestations of culture, thought, and history. We gratefully acknowledge the assistance and kindness of everyone at Crab Tree Farm, an extraordinary collection which has lent generously to the exhibition. Other lenders have been exceptionally helpful and enthusiastic, including Sarah Gage and Eric Turner at the Victoria and Albert Museum, London; Helen Batchelor at the National Railway Museum, York; and Veena Duncker; at the Royal Institute of British Architects, London, we would like to thank Catriona Cornelius and Eleanor Gawne; at the Richard Nickel Committee and Archive, Chicago, Ward Miller has been tremendously helpful, while John Vinci has kindly lent important Louis Sullivan fragments; at the David and Alfred Smart Museum of Art at The University of Chicago, many thanks go to Richard Born, Angela Steinmetz, and Natasha Derrickson; at the Frank Lloyd Wright Preservation Trust in Oak Park, Illinois, we sincerely thank Cheryl Bachand; we also thank Janet Parks of the Avery Architectural and Fine Arts Library at Columbia University; Eric Barnett at Southern Illinois University Edwardsville; Julian Hart and David Hart of Hart Gold & Silversmiths. At the Northwestern University Library, we would like to thank Scott Krafft for sharing the resources at the Charles Deering McCormick Library of Special Collections.

The catalogue would not be as richly illustrated without the many photographs by James Prinz. Roxanne Peters of the Victoria and Albert Museum has gone above and beyond to assist us with reproductions. The book seems to have taken shape once it was in the hands of designer Diane Jaroch, whose dedication and vision are seen on every page. We would like to thank the staff at Digital Collections, Northwestern University Library, for scans of imagery from the library's collections. We are grateful to Donna Shear and the staff at Northwestern University Press, which co-published the catalogue. Northwestern University Relations provided critical support to the project, especially editors Roseann Mark, Marianne Goss, Tom Frederickson, and Kingsley Day.

For their vital contributions to the project, thanks go out to interns Lindsay Amini, Ashley Carpenter, Daphne Palmer, and Irina Dykhne. Without the highly capable staff at the Block Museum, none of the various elements of this project would come to fruition. Thanks to Dan Silverstein, for clarity in his design and installation of the exhibition; Kristina Bottomley, for coordinating the loans from many sources; and Debora Wood, for her sound advice. Many thanks also to Amy Brandolino, Julia Csikesz, Paul Dougherty, Nicole Druckman, James Foster, Helen Hilken, Mary Hirsh, Burke Patten, Sheetal Prajapati, Will Schmenner, Laura Svedsen, and Carole Towns.

This far-reaching interdisciplinary project has been a model for the possibilities of university museums engaging students, faculty, and unique collections. Its interest, however, goes beyond the immediate university community. This publication, which will play a role in broadening the audience for the exhibition and extending its life, would never have come to light without the participation and support of the individuals and institutions listed above.

Corinne Granof
Curator

DESIGN IN THE AGE OF DARWIN: FROM WILLIAM MORRIS TO FRANK LLOYD WRIGHT

Stephen F. Eisenman

Preface

The title of this book and exhibition invokes a time when the theory and practice of design were closely tied to the theory of evolution. In the half-century following the 1859 publication of Darwin's *The Origin of Species*, the words "adaptation," "formalism," "fitness," "functionalism," and "type" were essential to architecture and design no less than to evolutionary biology, and their contested meanings underlay the programs and achievements of the artists discussed and presented here: William Morris, Christopher Dresser, C. R. Ashbee, C. F. A. Voysey, Louis Sullivan, and Frank Lloyd Wright. Their works and ideas in turn provided an essential foundation for 20th-century Modernism.

Introduction: Intelligent Design vs. Evolution by Natural Selection

Let's recall, to begin with, three important debates between Christian partisans of "intelligent design" and supporters of Darwinian evolutionism. The first dates to 1860, at the British Association for the Advancement of Science in Oxford, when Bishop Samuel Wilberforce, son of William, the great abolitionist, asked Thomas Huxley whether it was on the side of his grandmother or grandfather that he was descended from an ape. Huxley, known as Darwin's bulldog, replied that he would "rather have a miserable ape for a grandfather" than a man who would employ his faculties for the purpose of "introducing ridicule into a grave scientific discussion."[1] In fact, the debate at the British Association was more sophisticated than Huxley's retort suggests, and what evidence survives indicates that Wilberforce employed the best inductive reason and Victorian science to try to undermine the argument for transmutation. Nevertheless, the confrontation has been correctly taken as signaling the passage from a widespread theological to a new materialist outlook in the natural sciences, and indicating a new professionalism in scientific practice.

A second confrontation arose in 1925, at the famous "Monkey Trial" in Dayton, Tennessee, when John T. Scopes was charged with violating the Butler Act, which prohibited state employees from "teaching any theory that denies the story of the Divine creation of man as taught in the Bible, and to teach instead that man is descended from a lower order of animals."[2] Scopes was convicted and fined $100, but the victory of fundamentalism over science was Pyrrhic; history took the side of the agnostic Clarence Darrow over the evangelist William Jennings Bryan.[3]

The third debate occurred in 2000, when Christian fundamentalist voters in several mostly rural towns and districts in the United States elected school boards that added language to biology textbooks questioning the scientific validity of evolutionism and promoting "intelligent design." The verdict in Kitzmiller vs. Dover Pennsylvania School Board in December 2005, however, decisively rejected the teaching of intelligent design as an unconstitutional advancement of religion in a public school. The judge concluded: "To be sure, Darwin's theory of evolution is imperfect. However, the fact that a scientific theory can not yet render an explanation on every point should not be used as a pretext to thrust an untestable alternative hypothesis grounded in religion into the science classroom or to misrepresent well-established scientific propositions."[4]

Christopher Dresser, Textile (detail), 1871, James W. and C. Ward of Halifax, wool and silk. Collection of Crab Tree Farm.

1
"The Watch" (Plate 1), illustration by James Paxton from William Paley, *Natural Theology or, Evidences of the Existence and Attributes of the Deity collected from the Appearances of Nature* (Boston: Gould and Lincoln, 1869). The United Library of Garrett-Evangelical Theological Seminary and Seabury-Western Theological Seminary, Northwestern University.

The argument for intelligent design as the means by which nature achieved its diversity was first clearly put forward by the Reverend William Paley in his *Natural Theology* (1802), though it had a number of precedents, some ancient and medieval, including the last of Thomas Aquinas's Five Proofs of the Existence of God, from the *Summa Theologia* (1270).[5] Aquinas had argued that "natural bodies"—the sun, moon, and planets—act in consistent and predictable ways. But since these bodies "do not have intelligence and do not tend toward a result unless directed by someone knowing and intelligent (just as an arrow is sent by an archer)...there [must be] something intelligent by which all natural things are arranged in accordance with a plan—and this we call God."

Paley's arguments parallel the proof of Aquinas, being based on analogy and intended first of all to exalt God and only second to explain the complexity of the natural world. Just as the mechanism of a watch (Fig. 1), Paley claimed, is so exacting and refined as to require the existence of a watchmaker, the functioning of a bodily organ—for example, the human eye—is so complex and subtle that it proves the presence of an artificer, and that designer must be God.[6]

Paley's functionalist theology, like Aquinas's, was deemed "natural," since it began with an investigation of the material world and proceeded from that to revelation of the universal and divine. It was subsequently the intellectual basis for a series of apologetic tracts, the publication of which between 1833 and 1840 was supported by an endowment from Francis Egerton, Earl of Bridgewater. These well-known and widely distributed books—mockingly dubbed "the Bilgewater treatises" by Darwin and his circle—purported to explain the world's variety and complexity by means of natural theology and intelligent design. Charles Bell's particular contribution to the series, *The Hand, Its Mechanism and Vital Endowments as Evincing Design* (1833), was one of the most popular. It was read by both Darwin and John Ruskin and typifies the Bridgewater treatises in format and argumentation. Bell was an anatomist and surgeon and the author of an influential treatise on expression, *Essays on the Anatomy and Philosophy of Expression as Connected with the Fine Arts* (1844).[7] He began his Bridgewater book with the proposition—taken as self-evident—that the systematic arrangement of parts in any natural body offers evidence of intelligent design. He then moved on to consider the peculiar morphology of the human hand and its supreme fitness for diverse functions, concluding by remarking on its superiority to the comparable organ of any other species. An examination of the hand thus revealed both the beneficence of God and the exalted place of man in the great chain of being—what Bishop Wilberforce would later call the "golden chain of unsuspected relations which bind together all the mighty web which stretches from end to end of this full and most diversified earth."[8]

Darwin's theory of evolution by means of natural selection, by contrast, first published as a brief paper in the journal of the Linnean Society in 1858, then in book form in *The Origin of Species* of 1859, rejects any divine intervention in the appearance and disappearance of species or the design of organisms. It proposes that random variations or mutations in members of a species may render them more or less fit in the struggle for survival, and that those individuals better adapted to their environment or for reproduction will tend to survive and pass on favorable traits to their descendents, while those that are less advantaged will tend to die off. Over the vast expanse of geological time, small variations may be so magnified that whole new species emerge. Darwin accordingly illustrated his theory with a single plate (Fig. 2), a hypothetical evolutionary tree with numerous roots, trunks, and branches. It represents the principle of "divergence of character," the idea that when exaggerated over thousands of generations by the force of natural selection, small differences between individuals of a species—the latter are indicated by letters A to L at the bottom—will lead to greater and greater variations and eventually to the generation of distinct new species. By the ten-thousandth generation, Darwin suggests, a single species may have diverged into three others (designated on his graph as a10, f10, and m10), and thus become extinct. And from these three new species, still more may develop, each highly distinct from the original.

The implications of Darwin's theory remain today as powerful and disruptive to conservative politics and fundamentalist faith as ever before: that species have no essential being, and are instead nothing more than interbreeding populations that have a statistical likelihood of sharing certain characteristics; that mind is merely a function of brain and body; that humans have no inherently greater claim to life and the resources of nature than any other creature; that the past

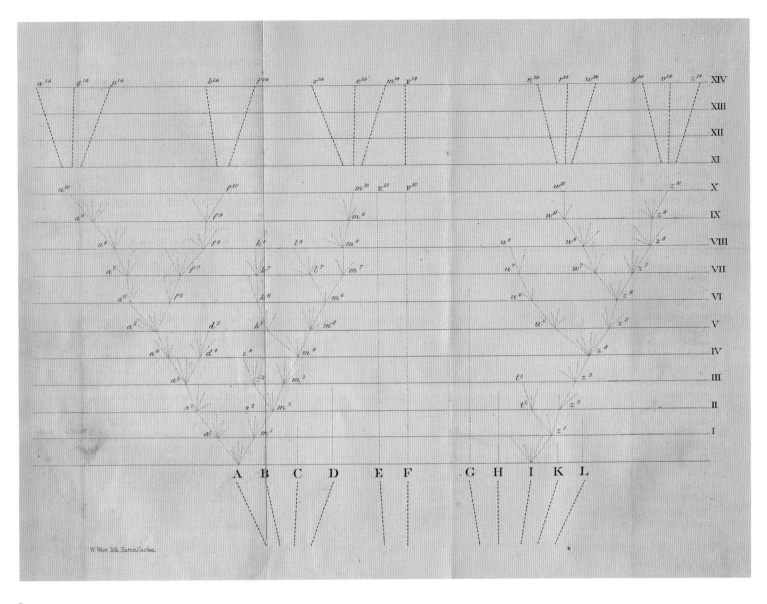

W West lith Hatton Garden.

2

Diagram illustrating "divergence of character, combined with principles of natural selection," from Charles Darwin, *On the Origin of Species by Means of Natural Selection* (London: John Murray, 1859). Charles Deering McCormick Library of Special Collections, Northwestern University Library.

and present have been shaped by struggle and contingency; and that the future remains an open question. Design is no less consequential a term for Darwin than for Paley, but for the evolutionist, it wholly lacked transcendence. According to Darwin, there was no "plan of creation," and no "unity of design," only the constant, heedless work of natural selection, crafting "prototypes," "structures," "patterns," and "variations." From a simple beginning, Darwin wrote, "endless forms most beautiful and most wonderful have been, and are being evolved."[9]

A conception of design, nevertheless, lay at the heart of evolutionary thought. Darwin's own use of the language of architecture and design, suggested by the quotations above, as well as his general debt to the theologian Paley and to comparative anatomists such as Bell, have been cogently discussed by Robert M. Young in his essay *Darwin's Metaphor* and by Stephen Jay Gould in his final book, *The Structure of Evolutionary Theory*.[10] Young makes clear that while Darwin saw no evidence of intelligent design in nature, he nevertheless employed a volitional language—selection, adaptation, and struggle—that gave ammunition to his critics (and erstwhile supporters) who, conceding the validity of evolution, insisted that there must be a divine agent that both set the process in motion and picked winners and losers. Natural selection, they argued, was simply not powerful enough or creative enough to construct such an elaborate web of life. This of course was Darwin's Achilles' heel, since he lived in an age before genetics and had no explanation for the mechanisms of mutation or the means of inheritance. Indeed, it was not until the period of the "modern synthesis" during the 1930s and 1940s when evolutionism and genetics were first integrated—and long after creationism was in retreat—that natural selection was generally accepted as the predominant force for evolutionary change.

But there were other early objections to natural selection beyond its apparent lack of creativity. Bishop Wilberforce, in his famous review of *The Origin of Species* from 1860, objected strenuously to the new deductive logic of Darwin's exposition, arguing that its lack of empirical verifiability violated a long and honored English tradition of Baconian induction. He argued, moreover, that the absence of evidence of transitional species in the fossil record cast doubt on the idea of evolution. To Darwin's reply, already outlined in the tenth chapter of *The Origin of Species*, that the fossil record was incomplete and that transitional species were by definition more transitory and thus less likely to leave fossil evidence, the bishop shook his head. Was Darwin arguing in a circle—using the theory of evolution ("transitional species") and natural selection to suggest why there was no direct evidence for his theory? Even Huxley admitted that Darwin's thesis could not be directly seen and proved. In fact, however, an account of the mechanism of mutation was unnecessary for Darwin's theory to stand. (Even today, mutation is a difficult matter to account for, though it is generally attributable to copying errors in the process of DNA replication and the effects of radiation, viruses, and other mutagens in the environment.) *How* variation occurred paled in significance beside the obvious fact *that* it occurred, and that organisms with beneficial adaptations tended to survive and have a greater chance of reproductive success.

Gould has argued that the very structure of Darwin's argument for natural selection and even his examples were based on Paley's "argument from design." Darwin and Paley were both functionalists, believing that plants and animals were specially adapted or designed to survive and prosper within corresponding environmental niches. But the naturalist radically undercut the theologian's propositions. Gould has written: "Nature features exquisite adaptation at overwhelming relative frequency…[but] this order, the very basis of Paley's inference about the nature of God, arises not directly from omnipotent benevolence, but only as a side consequence of a causal principle of entirely opposite import—namely, as the incidental effect of organisms struggling for their own benefit, expressed as reproductive success. Could any argument be more subversive?"[11] Darwin, in other words, overturned the very edifice of natural theology. Rather than demonstrating the perfection and omnipotence of the Creator, the "exquisite adaptation" of species to their environment proved the obverse: that the diversity of the myriad organisms of the natural world was the product of inanimate, blind, and impartial selective forces and mechanisms.

The Evolution of Design

In the age of Darwin—defined here as roughly half a century following publication of *The Origin of Species*—discussions of design were obviously not confined to theologians and biologists. In fact they were primarily, as one would expect during a period of industrial expansion, urbanization, and cultural modernization, the province of artists, planners, architects, and decorators. But theology and evolutionism stalked the discourses of fine art and decorative design just as much as design tracked evolution. Charles Bell's treatise on human expression is based on the idea that God specially endows humans with noble feelings unknown to animals and with facial muscles adapted to express these emotions. The evidence of this design is found both in anatomy and in great works of art—for example, the Hellenistic *Laocoön* and *Dying Gaul*. Bell says of the former that he suffers in noble silence. "The artist's design was to show corporeal exertion, the attitudes and struggles of the body and of the arms. The throat is inflated, the chest straining to give power to the muscles of the arms, while the slightly parted lips show that no breath escapes, or at most, a low hollow groan."[12]

But it was in the domain of the decorative arts rather than painting and sculpture that evolutionism and theology were most intertwined. In 1852 the architect and art historian Matthew Digby Wyatt, who served as secretary of the Great Exhibition in London and later as the first Slade Professor at Cambridge University, began his survey of the marvels on display in the Crystal Palace by writing: "It has pleased the beneficent Designer of the world and all that therein is, not only to surround man with the ever-varying and inexhaustible beauties of nature, and to endow him with the gift of sight to perceive her graces; but he has been pleased also to confer upon him a mind to understand, and a hand to imitate them."[13] The new products of manufactures and industry, he further argued, and the principle of "mechanical repetition" were the ordained expressions of the age.[14] Here Wyatt, like Bell before him, sees the work of human design and natural creation as working in concert: Each reciprocally proves the wisdom and benevolence of God; each affirms as well the genius of the British Empire and industry and exalts the royal patrons of the Crystal Palace exhibition, Queen Victoria and Prince Albert.

In the same year, the American sculptor and critic Horatio Greenough expressed his wonderment at the world's extraordinary variety of plant and animal forms and their obedience to a "law of adaptation." The same law, he believed, must govern architecture and design: "If there be any principle of structure more plainly inculcated in the works of the Creator than all others, it is the principle of unflinching adaptation of forms to functions."[15] (A few decades later, architect Louis Sullivan would dispense with God and simply state that "form follows function.") And at the end of our period, in 1909, when supporters of intelligent design were in retreat and evolutionism was the reigning paradigm, the English architect and designer C. F. A. Voysey, in an essay called "Ideas in Things," tried to reconcile religion and science. He repeatedly claimed that the goal of the Arts and Crafts Movement was to restore to human life the spiritual realm that had been sacrificed on the altar of rampant materialism. Functional design and fine handcraft, such as Voysey employed in 1898 for Arthur Currier Briggs (wealthy son of a colliery owner) at the rural retreat called Broadleys (see plate 38) on Lake Windermere in Cumbria, were the best means to that restoration. Here the architect fashioned everything from iron chimney pieces, window pulls, and door knobs to its three enormous bow windows, placed to permit panoramic views of Lake Windermere. The same attention to the details of form and function was manifested at the Pastures in Leicestershire for Miss G. C. Conant, with its specially designed dovecote (Fig. 3) "Fitness," he wrote, in homage to Paley, Darwin, evolutionism, and a generation of functionalist architects and theorists, "is a universal law of nature."[16]

Ideas about fitness and evolution in design, of course, long predated Darwin or Voysey, as the architectural historian Peter Collins has shown.[17] The idea that architecture and ornament evolved or developed over time and progressed by increasingly sophisticated adaptations to the body, the environment, and functional necessity had for generations been constitutive of its history, theory, and practice. It is exemplified, to begin with, by the analogies made between architec-

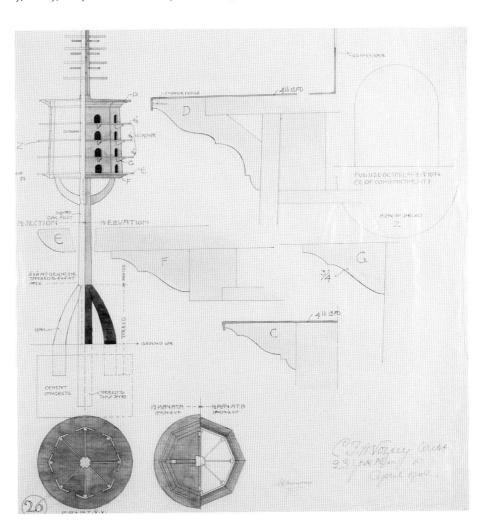

3
C. F. A. Voysey, *Design for a Dovecote for Miss G. C. Conant, North Luffenham, Leicestershire: The Pastures*, 1902, wash on linen. RIBA Library Drawings & Archives Collections SB110/ Voy [109](5).

4
"Public Conduits," in A. Welby
Pugin, *Contrasts or A Parallel
Between the Noble Edifices
of the Fourteenth and Fifteenth
Centuries and Similar Build-
ings of the Present Day
Showing the Present Decay
of Taste* (London, 1836).
Charles Deering McCormick
Library of Special Collections,
Northwestern University
Library.

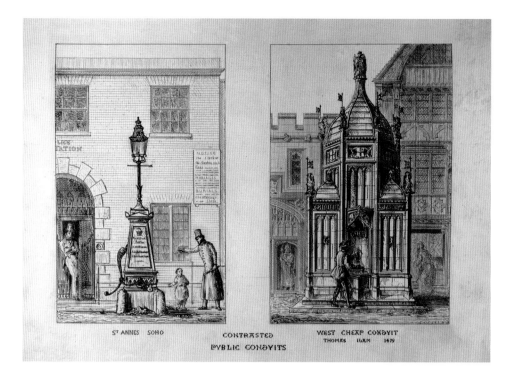

ST ANNES SOHO   CONTRASTED   WEST CHEAP CONDVIT

PVBLIC CONDVITS   THOMAS ILLAM 1479

ture and the proportions of the human body (anthropomorphism) in the work and writings of Renaissance Italians Leon-Battista Alberti, Francesco di Giorgio, and Antonio Palladio. It is also evident in the concept of architectural decorum or appropriateness derived from the Roman writer
and architect Vitruvius (and revived during the Renaissance by Alberti), which proposed that a
building be designed in such a way that its form be inextricably tied to its environment, site, and
function as well as the social status of the user.

     Adaptation was central to the thought of the English 19th-century Gothic revivalist Augus-
tus Welby Pugin, who, for all his appeals to the supposed timeless values of a medieval Christian
age of charity and community, argued in his *Contrasts* (1841) that "the great test of Architectural
beauty is the fitness of the design to the purpose for which it is intended, and that the style of the
building should so correspond with its use that the spectator may at once perceive the purpose for
which it was erected"[18] (Fig. 4). He further argued that the mind of the craftsmen who design and
build noble Christian edifices must be "imbued with devotion for, and faith in, the religion for
whose worship they were erected."[19] In other words, the laborer himself must be spiritually adapted to the task at hand and undertake it with true Christian feeling if the results are to be noble.

     For Pugin's great follower, the critic, artist, and moralist John Ruskin, historical (epochal)
fitness and adaptation were also important. Every age had its own style precisely suited to contemporaneous moral and political standards. "The art of any country," Ruskin wrote "is the exponent
of its social and political virtues. The art, or general productive and formative energy of any country
is an exact exponent of its ethical life. You can have a noble art only from noble persons, associated
under laws fitted to their time and circumstances."[20] In *The Two Paths* (1859) Ruskin wrote, that the
"moral character" of a culture and the nature of a civilization could be adjudged by its art.[21] It was
precisely this attention to the mutability of historical styles and their succession—instead of to
more purely aesthetic qualities—that so incensed the critic Geoffrey Scott in 1914 and led him to
condemn the impact of "the philosophy of evolution" on architectural practice.[22] In *The Architecture
of Humanism*, Scott wrote: "The object of evolutionary criticism is not to appreciate but to explain....
The most odious characteristics of an art become convenient evidences of heredity and environment, by means of which every object can be duly set in a grand and luminous perspective."[23]

     But neither Pugin nor Ruskin was among the principal apologists for an evolutionary the-
ory of architecture and design; that distinction would be held by the mid-19th-century architects
and writers Eugène Emmanuel Viollet-le-Duc in France, James Fergusson in England, and Gottfried
Semper in Germany and Austria. (Semper was also highly influential in England from 1850 to 1855;
after the success of the Great Exhibition of 1851, he encouraged the formation of a new Museum
of Manufactures, which eventually became the Victoria and Albert Museum.) Each of these men

argued that the evolution of architecture was the result of functional adaptations to particular environments, a long history of trial and error, and a process of what may be called "artificial selection." Those architectural or design solutions that best satisfied needs and functions at particular times were selected by patrons and communities for survival, while those that did not were cast aside. Viollet-le-Duc in 1854 described Gothic architecture as an organism "which develops and progresses as nature does in the creation of beings; starting from a very simple principle which it then modifies, which it perfects, which it makes more complicated, but without ever destroying the original essence."[24] The French architect's doctrine is in fact a hybrid of evolutionary functionalism and formalism—the former evidenced by the architect's remarks about architectural adaptation and perfectibility, and the latter by his idea that the "original essence" of both nature and design is preserved in the course of any evolutionary progress or change. The distinction, we shall discover, lay at the heart of British and American design debates for much of the latter half of the 19th century.

Fergusson, in a chapter titled "Progress in Art" from his book *An Historical Enquiry into the True Principles of Beauty in Art* (1849), wrote that the development of ecclesiastical architecture from the 12th through 14th centuries was marked by "a series of buildings one succeeding the other, and the last containing not only all the improvements before introduced into all the former examples, but contributing something new toward perfecting a style."[25] The history of architecture was thus a constant unfolding, each major edifice built upon an earlier achievement, but nevertheless guided by functional necessity. Viollet-le-Duc's and Fergusson's evolutionism was inspired by, among others, Thomas Malthus, Erasmus Darwin, Georges Cuvier, and J. B. Lamarck, and was correspondingly non-Darwinian by virtue of its emphasis on the inevitability of architectural progress or improvement. It was not Darwin but the radical transmutationist Lamarck who argued that the use or disuse of a limb or organ correspondingly strengthened or weakened it, and that these acquired traits could be inherited. Fergusson's later work on Buddhist temples however, as Huxley noticed, was profoundly influenced by the Darwinian theory of natural selection.[26] He insisted that the correspondence of architectural and social developments could be seen with clarity especially in India because of its great variety of distinctive peoples and faiths. Thus India was a social and design laboratory where great numbers of specimens all competed against one another, with the fittest fated to survive and pass on its particular traits.

In his vast and ambitious study of the history and theory of ornament, *Der Stil* (1860–63), Semper argued that new artistic forms and materials revealed vestiges of earlier ones. (The idea may have been inspired by Robert Chambers's sensational book of 1844, *Vestiges of the Natural History of Creation*, which proposed a theory of evolution and extinction partly derived from Lamarck.) The geometric decoration on a piece of ceramic used for containing water, to cite a single example, was likely a transmutation of the tightly woven pattern of baskets that formerly served the same function. Decorative schemes, Semper said, contained a visualized memory of primitive symbolic elements—for example, the banding around the neck of a vase or the ornamental frieze around the upper story of a building may have been derived from primordial wreaths used to crown the brows of heroic warriors or athletes. Most of all, style was the artistic adaptation of a preexisting form to its material, technical, environmental, and cultural circumstance, permitting the gradual progress and development of architecture and design. All present forms were derived from a few primal elements of building and design—ceramic, textile, solid geometry, carpentry—adapted to local circumstances. In a lecture delivered in 1869, he proposed that "building styles… are not invented, but develop in various departures from a few primitive types, according to the laws of natural breeding, of transmission, and adaptation. Thus the development is similar to the evolutions in the province of organic creation."[27] In his emphasis on gradual development and improvement, Semper, like Viollet-le-Duc, may have been invoking uniformitarianism, the doctrine of the British geologist (and supporter of Darwin) Charles Lyell, who argued that the same slow-acting forces that shaped the earth in the past were still operative in the present. But this was as far as Semper would go in his embrace of Darwinism. He rejected what he saw as the determinism of natural selection and its restrictions on the free will of the artist or designer. Indeed, the purpose of the lecture cited above was the refutation of what he saw as the pernicious influence of Darwin on design: "We can quite rightly describe the old monuments as the fossilized receptacles of extinct social organizations, but these did not grow on the backs of society like shells on the backs of snails, nor did they spring forth from blind natural process like coral reefs. They are the free creations of man."[28]

The evolutionism of Ruskin, Viollet-le-Duc, Fergusson, and Semper did not, as we have seen, directly derive from the work of Darwin or from the theory of natural selection. It was instead the continuation of a long tradition of evolutionary thought, as well as a response to contemporary challenges posed by numerous French and British biologists and naturalists. However, the work and writings of the British and American designers and architects highlighted in the exhibition—Christopher Dresser, William Morris, C. F. A. Voysey, C. R. Ashbee, Louis Sullivan, and Frank Lloyd Wright—were conceived and developed to a significant degree in response to the Darwinian challenge, if not explicitly to Darwin himself. Their works and careers constitute the terms of an implicit debate concerning the question of evolution and natural selection in the practice and theory of the decorative arts. The argument among these figures would prove highly consequential for the development of 20th-century Modernism, with its alternate embrace of handcraft and machine production, its aversion to ornament, and especially its theories of functionalism and types or typology. It was an argument ultimately informed by issues of class, labor, and power as much as by science.

Recall here that the principle of architectural or design fitness or adaptation—of form following function—became especially important in England during a period of accelerated industrialization and economic growth in the wake of the Chartist upsurge of 1848. (Chartism was the first great working-class movement in modern England. It lasted from 1838 to 1848 and took its name from the People's Charter of 1838, a petition of grievance that described a needed democratic reform of voting. The movement ended with a failed mass rally in 1848, modest political concessions, and an economic upturn after 1850.) For the first time, architectural adaptation was no longer conceived in Vitruvian terms, as a matter of matching, say, an elevated style or rhetoric to a suitably exalted patron or function; it was instead understood in evolutionary terms, to be the expression of economical methods of construction or manufacture and the efficient utilization of materials and labor power. Architecture and design, many writers argued, were no longer embedded in particular styles such as Gothic or Renaissance, but were instead the pure products of modern engineering and mass-produced materials—iron, glass, terra cotta, brick, concrete—adapted to new programs and functions, such as railway bridges and stations, canals, exhibition halls, and department stores. Indeed, the question of an appropriate architectural and design style, it was increasingly believed, could best be settled (like any other practical question) by competition, laissez-faire, and the pursuit of efficiency.[29] The English mathematician and engineer Charles Babbage provided a key economic component of the theory underlying architectural rationalism and natural selection alike. In 1832 he argued that dividing any manufacturing process into discrete tasks and selecting workers according to their skill levels had the effect of lowering labor costs and speeding work. He wrote: "The master manufacturer, by dividing the work to be executed into different processes, each requiring different degrees of skill or force, can purchase exactly that precise quantity of both which is necessary for each process; whereas if the whole work were executed by one workman, that person must possess sufficient skill to perform the most difficult, and sufficient strength to execute the most laborious, of the operations into which the art is divided." In short, to divide the manufacturing process lowers the cost of labor and quickens the accomplishment of the work.

Darwin employed essentially the same idea in the pivotal fourth chapter in *The Origin of Species,* "Natural Selection," when he discussed both the selective advantages of sexual dimorphism in plants and the benefits of the differential physiologies of pollinating insects. He wrote: "No naturalist doubts the advantage of what has been called 'the physiological division of labor;' hence we may believe that it would be advantageous to a plant to produce stamens alone in one flower…and pistils alone in another." The same principle operates with pollinators and nectar-feeding insects, which are able to obtain advantages by developing, through natural selection, physiologies precisely suited to helping them gain access to the sexual parts of particular plants. Darwin's description might have been one given by an industrial designer proudly exhibiting his latest products or newest machines at the Crystal Palace exhibition:

I could give many facts showing how anxious bees are to save time: for instance, their habit of cutting holes and sucking the nectar at the bases of certain flowers, which with a very little more trouble, they can enter by the mouth. Bearing such facts in mind, it may be believed that under certain circumstances individual differences in the curvature or length of the proboscis, etc., too slight to be appreciated by us, might profit a bee or other insect, so that certain individuals would be able to obtain their food more quickly than others; and thus the communities to which they belonged would flourish and throw off many swarms inheriting the same peculiarities."[30]

And this is where ideology, politics, power, and social class intrude upon the province of pure science: What is good for the bees may not be so good for the humans. The industrial division and subdivision of labor in 19th-century England depressed wages, eroded means of livelihood, and encouraged degradation of the skill and knowledge of workers, who were no longer able to understand a manufacturing process from beginning to end.[31] This simultaneous maximization of labor productivity and degradation of work, accompanied by a wider technological rationalism, led to generations of social and political struggle and formed the ideological subtext for architectural and design debates for generations to come. The contest between the typological (formalist or structuralist) design style of Christopher Dresser, which depended on an elaborated division of labor, and the more individualistic and skills-based approach of William Morris and his followers was thus a contest between different visions of social and industrial as well as biological evolution and development. A dispute in one domain implicitly entailed a dispute in the other; a disagreement over design and evolution was a disagreement about the proper organization of social and political life. This was especially the case, as historian Adrian Desmond has argued, in the generation before Darwin, though it continued to be salient in the generation after.[32] (Darwin's own struggle with the radical political implications of his theory, which caused him to delay publication of *The Origin of Species* for nearly 25 years, is a case in point.) But whatever parallels existed in the 1860s and 1870s between Dresser, formalism, and an elaborated industrial division of labor, and between Morris, functionalism, and a skills-based approach to craft production, broke down by the generation of Voysey, Ashbee, Sullivan, and Wright. In the last decade of the 19th century and the first two decades of the 20th, formalism was increasingly viewed as a radical democratizing approach to architecture and design, and the Arts and Crafts movement as the buttress of a new, more manly nationalism, embraced by a modernizing rural gentry or an emergent leisure class that made its money in industry and finance.

Morris vs. Dresser (Functionalism vs. Formalism)

William Morris, along with a number of his Arts and Crafts followers, represents one side of the debate concerning the evolution of design. His position is materialist, functionalist, and generally compatible with the mainstream of British scientific thinkers—from Robert Boyle in the 17th century to Richard Dawkins in the 21st—who have argued that the morphology of an organism derives from what Darwin called its "conditions of existence"—that is, from adaptation to the varied circumstances of life. Morris described the development of society and the evolution of ornament as the result of historical processes shaped by adaptation, struggle, and sheer accident or contingency, and he correspondingly embraced the idea that chance provided a basis for the depiction of plants and animals. That is, he believed that the conditional appearance of organisms—the way a plant or animal looked at particular times and determined places, not their idealized or stylized form—was the appropriate foundation for their representation in flat patterns or three dimensions. This emphasis on the contingent aspect of individual plant and animal morphology—one of the essential features of a Darwinian paradigm that views more or less random mutation as the raw material of natural selection and evolution—is seen, for example, in wallpaper designs from early and late in his career, such as *Fruit* (or *Pomegranate*) and *Willow Boughs* (see plates 21 and 22), in which leaves twist or curl as they would in nature, according to the effects of mutation or the impact of sun, wind, and rain. The affinity here, it should be stressed, is conceptual, not formal; there is little actual resemblance between the highly schematic or diagrammatic illustrations found, for example, in Darwin's *The Movements and Habits of Climbing Plants* (Fig. 5) and Morris's

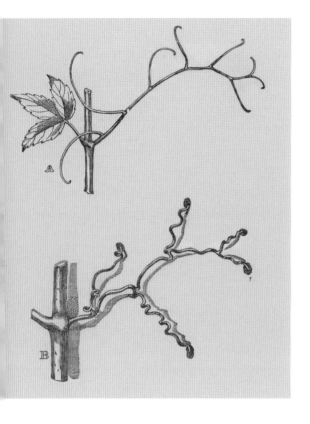

5
"Ampelopsis hederacea
[Virginia Creeper]" (Fig. 11),
illustration by George
Darwin in Charles Darwin,
*The Movement and Habits
of Climbing Plants*, second
edition (New York: D. Apple-
ton and Company, 1876),
Northwestern University
Library.

6
William Morris, *Willow
Boughs* (wallpaper), 1887,
(see plate 22). Collection
of Crab Tree Farm.

Willow Boughs (Fig. 6). But there is a shared concern with movement, animation, adaptation, and contingency. In addition, many of Morris's textile designs, including his *Hammersmith* rugs and the silk velvet brocade *Granada*, display the combined vestiges of several past ornamental styles—Persian, Indian, Celtic, Gothic, Renaissance—suggesting that they were the product of evolutionary history, not the manifestation of a single ideal and unchanging ornamental type. (The latter per-spective is represented by Owen Jones's 1868 book *The Grammar of Ornament*, which sought to reveal the "general laws" that underlay each historical phase in the development of ornamental art from "Savage Tribes" to the "Italian Ornament" of the 16th century.[33]) Morris's *Hammersmith* rug (Fig. 7), for example, is based in part on 16th-century Florentine velvets employing ogival pome-granate designs, but it has a two-dimensional integrity that also recalls Persian carpets such as the great Ardabil carpets (1539–40) in the Los Angeles County Museum and the Victoria and Albert Museum (Fig. 8). (The V & A carpet was acquired on the recommendation of Morris.)

The furnishings produced by Morris & Co., a firm established in 1861 at no. 8 Red Lion Square in London, are likewise an amalgam of many historical styles including Gothic, Baroque, and even Egyptian. Indeed, the most famous furniture design to come from the Morris studios, the "Sussex" range of rush-seated settles and chairs (Fig. 9), derives from indigenous or vernacular English chairs, Regency prototypes, and Japanese bamboo furnishings. Morris's early business manager, Warrington Taylor, went so far as to deny that the furniture had any style at all: "Red Lion Square furniture has no style; modern work must only be founded on nature, severity, and true construction. There must be no notion of precedent, fashion, century."[34] For Morris & Co., a strict commitment to function as well as receptiveness to the facts and beauty of nature—not precon-ceived or idealized types or styles—were the foundations of modern design. "Have nothing in your house," Morris wrote, "that you do not know to be useful or believe to be beautiful."

The botanist and industrial designer Christopher Dresser represents the second major and contrasting direction in mid- and late 19th-century design practice and theory. His position was idealist, formalist, structuralist, and broadly in line with the thought of Continental scientists, including Etienne Geoffroy Saint-Hilaire, Johann Wolfgang von Goethe, and the German botanist Alexander Braun, who argued (as Darwin summarized) that there was a unity of form in nature, "a fundamental agreement in structure [among] beings of the same class, which is quite independent of their habits of life."[35] For formalists such as Dresser (Fig. 10), all plants were deeply homologous with each other, governed by strict rules of architecture, structure, and design, and shaped by com-mon laws of growth. He also saw societies and cultures as essentially static and possessing a sin-

7
William Morris, *Rug*, ca. 1880,
Morris & Co., wool,
Collection of Crab Tree Farm.

8
Anonymous, Maqsud of Kashan,
Iran, *Ardabil Carpet*, 1539–40.
Victoria and Albert Museum,
London, 272-1983.

9
Philip Webb, *Sussex Armchair*,
ca. 1865, Morris & Co.,
ebonized beech with rush.
Victoria and Albert Museum,
London, Circ.288-1960.

10
Christopher Dresser, Drawing
from a Pedagogical Album,
1854–56, ink and watercolor
on paper, Victoria and Albert
Museum, London, 3979.

11
"Skeleton, or Old Bogey"
(Fig. 22), in Christopher
Dresser, *Principles of Decora-
tive Design* (London: Cassell,
Peter, & Galpin , 1873).
Charles Deering McCormick
Library of Special Collections,
Northwestern University
Library.

12
Christopher Dresser, *Caneware Vase*, 1867, Wedgwood,
ceramic. Private collection.

13
"Vertebra of lungfish and
salamander (fig. 101)," in
Richard Owen, *On the Anatomy of Vertebrates*, vol. 1,
(Longmans, Green, and Co.,
1866). Northwestern University Library.

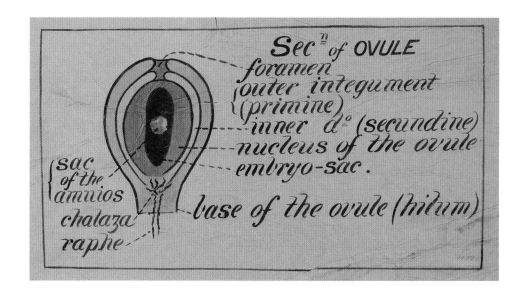

gle timeless character (though his attitude toward Japan, where he traveled in 1876 and 1877, was significantly more nuanced). And correspondingly, like most botanists of his day as well as his teachers Owen Jones and Gottfried Semper, he largely rejected Darwinian and other historical and materialist theories of speciation and descent. But Dresser was not a dogmatist; he accepted and even embraced many elements of functionalist thought, but without moving into the opposite camp. Therefore, like Semper and Jones, Dresser found himself locked in a tight embrace with evolution and adaptation, striving on the one hand to prove that all plants conformed to determined Linnean archetypes, and on the other recognizing, and indeed championing, the idea that the adaptation of form to function—a process, after all, that unfolds historically—was the very foundation of modern industry and design.

At times this split led Dresser to devise an ornamentation that was both generic and idiosyncratic, formalist, and sui generis, created, it seemed, by a resourceful but capricious God. Examples of this include the many patterns from his 1873 book *Principles of Decorative Design* (Fig. 11) illustrating "the power of ornament to express feelings": some of his ceramics, including a Wedgwood *Caneware Vase* (Fig. 12) featuring motifs derived from bird and fish bones such as those illustrated in Richard Owen's *Anatomy of Vertebrates* (1866) (Fig. 13), and numerous Minton tiles with stylized acanthus leaves, wagon wheels, and saw-tooth patterns.[36] His Romantic perspective is derived in significant part from Goethe, whose *Metamorphosis of Plants* (1790) he read with care and wrote about in a scholarly article in 1861. Dresser, like Goethe, believed the design of plants and their development to be the consequence of internal and highly predictable laws of transformation and growth, dictated by the waxing and waning of their "vital forces."[37] In a letter to Johann Gottfried von Herder, Goethe—in words that anticipate those of an industrial designer—described the myriad inventions made possible by the discovery of the archetype:

The archetypal plant as I see it will be the most wonderful creation in the world, and nature herself will envy me for it. With this model, and the key to it, one will be able to invent plants...which, even if they do not actually exist, nevertheless might exist, and which are not merely picturesque or poetic visions and illusions, but have inner truth and logic. The same law will permit itself to be applied to everything that is living.[38]

The perspective is Promethian—or more aptly, Faustian!—and appropriate for a dawning age of industry that placed unprecedented value on models, prototypes, templates, and infinite repeatability. All that was missing from Goethe's account—and what was provided by Dresser and others involved in the South Kensington system of drawing and design instruction—was an actual mechanism for adapting the myriad variations of the archetype to the particular needs of manufacture and use. Thus it is necessary in discussing Dresser to reverse the Darwinian (and later Sullivanian) aphorism and say that for him, "function ever follows form," as revealed by even a glimpse at Dresser's strange and even bizarre Clutha (cloudy) glassware for James Couper & Sons (see plates 8 and 9) and his ceramics for the Linthorpe and Ault potteries (see plates 6 and 7), espe-cially the *Goat Vase* and *Tongue Vase*.

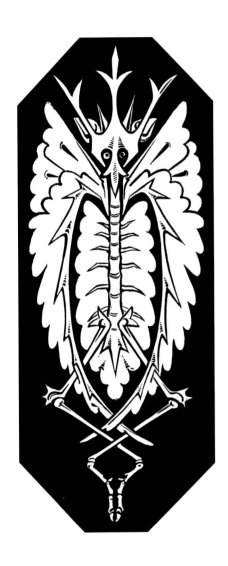

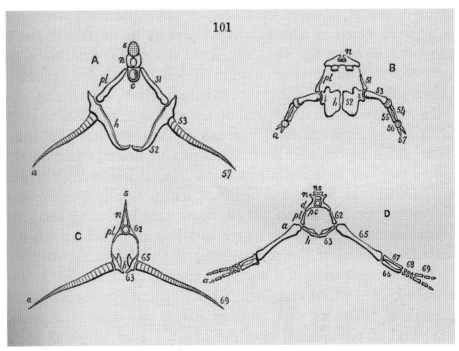

101

Dresser thus paradoxically provided a resource for Art Nouveau artists, including Voysey, Ashbee, and Arthur Mackmurdo, who positively trumpeted contingency, dynamism, and at times the uncanny, in their designs and made significant use of industrial technology as well. Unlike Morris, Voysey made no effort to mask the pattern of repeats in most of his wallpapers, as in *Bird, Fruit, Flowers* and *Vine and Bird* (see plates 36 and 37), and indeed relished the sense of movement and vitality they induced, as visible in *Snakes among Weed* (see page 65). That energy may also be seen in Mackmurdo's famous cover designs for *Wren's City Churches* (Fig. 14), sometimes regarded as the very first Art Nouveau invention, and the deluxe magazine *The Hobby Horse* (Fig. 15), published by the Century Guild. In fact, Mackmurdo was a Neo-Lamarckian who also deeply admired the works of Herbert Spencer (coiner of the term "survival of the fittest"); he believed that art, manufactures, and nature were alike in their tendency to progress, with each stage of development always superseded by new forms better adapted to a changed environment.[39]

William Morris and Evolutionary Anthropology

There is no evidence that Morris ever met Darwin or even read his works, though given his curiosity and erudition, it would be very surprising if he did not have at least some familiarity with them. All the same, the only explicit reference I have found to Morris's views on Darwin is his daughter May's comment that the scientist "would have been in every way outside the scope of Morris's list" [of favorite authors], because he [Morris] concurred with Ruskin's view that "it is every man's duty to know what he *is* and not to think of the embryo he was, nor the skeleton that he shall be."[40] In this instance, however, the daughter probably misunderstood her father's mind. While Morris bitterly disdained social Darwinism, in particular Spencer's 1884 paean to the laws of supply and demand, *Man Versus the State* (Morris said the book most of all upheld the "freedom of fleecing"), he embraced evolutionism in almost all his mature writings and, as I have already begun to suggest, in his art as well.[41] At the same time, he rejected some key elements of Darwinian theory—in particular, its historical linearity and its apparent Malthusianism.

By 1885 Morris had read Friedrich Engels's *The Origin of the Family, Private Property and the State*, published the previous year, as well as writings by the anthropologists Lewis Henry Morgan, E. B. Tylor, and Henry Sumner Maine, among others.[42] These men were prominent evolutionists who argued, roughly, that the development of human society was the consequence of material and historical, rather than supernatural, factors; that societies progressed from rude, or savage, origins to modern enlightenment; and that traces, or "survivals," of the remote past are frequently apparent in the contemporary cultural record. Morris absorbed a great deal of evolutionary thought—including its tripartite division of human history into epochs of Savagery, Barbarism, and Civilization—and discussed it in such works as *Socialism from the Root Up* (1886) and *Socialism—Its Growth and Outcome* (1893). Near the beginning of the latter work, Morris specifically approved the writings of Lewis Henry Morgan and the doctrine of "social evolution" and spoke of the need to regard society "from its dynamic aspect, as the agent and patient of change."[43] But Morris was unlike most evolutionary anthropologists of his day in two respects. First, far from disparaging the so-called Barbaric past as a time of ignorance, superstition, promiscuity, and violence, he saw it as a golden age of abundance, reciprocity, pleasurable labor, gender equality, and communalism; and second, rather than envisioning history as a straight path from the past to the present, he saw it configured like a spiral. Every distinct crossroads of human history—marked by signal developments in the mode of production and distinct stages of the class struggle—entailed a reprise or reappearance of certain ideological and material structures from the past, albeit adapted to changed conditions. This model of development and adaptation—figured, we might say, in spiral patterns derived from botany or hydrology, as in Morris's cotton patterns *Evenlode*, *Cray* (Fig. 16), and *Wandle* (see plate 20), named after rivers of England—suggests that significant aspects of early history and social organization might be restored in the future. The principle is functionalist by virtue of its suggestion that ancient forms, traditions, and practices may be engaged to serve modern needs, but is nevertheless anti-Darwinian. For the scientist, as his evolutionary tree illustrated, there is no going back; a medieval revivalist like Morris could never be fully Darwinian in outlook, though his embrace of the concept of survivals is consistent with the idea that present homologies are the evolutionary vestiges of past adaptations. His printed, woven, and embroidered two-dimensional patterns are thus figurations of history, progress, survival, and change as much as they are idealized representations of particularly loved leaves, branches, flowers, fruits, and rivers.

Although Morris's wallpaper, cotton, and wool designs were derived from the close observation of nature in all its contingent aspects, they also were drawn, as already indicated, from a great variety of historical sources: late medieval and early modern English, French, and German manuscripts and incunabula, as well as more exotic sources, including silks and cottons from Mughal India, Japanese enamels, and Icelandic embroideries from the 14th century and later. In addition, Morris used anachronistic reproductive and craft technologies. His papers were printed by hand from wooden blocks, and his dyes, brewed in wooden barrels or vats, were made from recipes found in Renaissance herbals. Moreover, his designs were products of only a minimal division of labor: Morris fully executed his two-dimensional patterns instead of simply sketching outlines and handing them to draftsmen. This latter was often Dresser's approach, as is apparent in notebooks such as the one at the Ipswich Museum and in the few surviving sketches he made that outlined new patterns.

In thus embracing the styles, forms, and even technologies of the past, Morris was attempting to restore to memory the pleasure, communal character, and sheer ingenuity of previous art. His focus in particular upon the design (and also the literature) of the late 14th century—the period of the English Peasants' Revolt—was a consequence of his conviction that the revolutionary sentiments of that distant era had never been chased from the national character. They were cultural "survivals"—this is Morris's word, derived from the evolutionary anthropologist Tylor—restored to consciousness and given new functions during the latest period of labor organization and political agitation. Morris's art and design were thus intended to revive a long-suppressed desire for emancipation, a theme represented in his novel *A Dream of John Ball* (1888), with its frontispiece

etching by Edward Burne-Jones (Fig. 17) whose inscription announces that labor discipline and bosses are modern inventions: "When Adam Delved and Eve Span/Who Was Then the Gentleman." We might say that Morris and his comrades and followers—including Voysey and Ashbee—selected and adapted medieval and other exotic styles in the belief that they fit within a political and ideo-logical niche that appeared with rapid industrialization and the later-19th-century rise of the British labor movement and international socialism. And even though he accepted Marx's dictum that the history of society is the history of class struggle, he did not believe, with Malthus, Darwin, and Spencer, that want and competition were built into both human and external nature. Indeed, it was Morris's association of natural selection with the individualism and competitiveness of the capital-ist marketplace and bourgeois society that led him to hold Darwin at arm's length despite his undoubted debt to the thinker.

Christopher Dresser and the Idea of Type

Christopher Dresser developed his design practice and theory in the very shadow of Darwin. He was a highly skilled botanist, receiving a PhD in absentia from the University of Jena in 1859, and was a trusted colleague of Darwin's close friend Joseph Hooker, then assistant director of the Royal Botanic Gardens, Kew. Hooker soon succeeded his father as director at Kew, and in 1861 both men sponsored Dresser for membership in the prestigious Linnean Society. Beginning in 1857, however, Dresser regularly attended meetings and delivered papers at the society. Although a recent exami-nation of Linnean Society minutes and attendance records reveals that Dresser was not in the audience when Wallace's and Darwin's epochal papers *On the Tendency of Species to Form Vari-eties* and *On the Perpetuation of Varieties and Species by Means of Natural Selection* were present-ed to the society in 1858 by its secretary, he must have read them soon after, since his own essay, "Contributions to Organographic Botany," was published in the same volume of the *Journal of the Proceedings of the Linnean Society* as those of the two then notorious "transmutationists."[44] In addition, Dresser's essay "Stem and Leaf and their Transmutation" was published in *The Regis-ter of Facts and Occurrences Relating to Literature, the Sciences and the Arts* just a few months after the same periodical devoted eight double-column pages to "the *Origin of Species* controversy."[45] It is reasonable to suppose he was a regular reader of the journal that published one of his most ambitious scholarly articles, one that asserted (contra Goethe) that the stem preceded the leaf as the base material out of which the rest of the plant developed.

Though he addressed "transmutation" in the article just cited—"all parts of a plant are modifications either of the leaf or the stem"—Dresser's definition of the term precluded the muta-bility of species.[46] What he meant by transmutation was the modification or development of an individual specimen in the course of its life cycle, as first outlined by Goethe in his *Metamorphosis of Plants* (1790). Indeed, Dresser's books on plant morphology positively trumpeted the perma-nence of species, as well as the logic and regularity of form. These monographs are organized around three basic premises: 1) that there is a single common structure fundamental to all plants; 2) that every plant species has an underlying unvarying morphology, even if that ideal form is invis-ible in any particular specimen; and 3) that a coherence exists between the part and the whole of a specimen.

These principles are derived from several Continental and British sources. The philoso-pher Immanuel Kant's idea of the reciprocity of part/whole in the *Prolegomena to Any Future Meta-physics* certainly undergirded Dresser's positions, though more proximate, specifically biological sources may be identified. The French scientist Georges Cuvier, whose writings, along with those of his Swedish predecessor Carolus Linneus, were familiar to every botanist of Dresser's day, had similarly argued that "types," or the ideal configuration of forms and relations constituting the basis of an organism, were inalterable, possessing the same consistency, for example, as abstract figures of plane geometry. And just as geometric forms could be used to generate equations that revealed essential properties of the figures themselves and their derivatives, so types could be used to study specific organisms and their variations. Goethe's position, outlined in his letter to Herder cited above, was quite similar.

Typology was thus the basis of comparative morphology, the new branch of biology, practiced by Darwin's nemesis Richard Owen and by Dresser himself, that was concerned with recognizing homologies—similarities of form, structure, and function among species—in the belief that these exposed underlying patterns or unities in nature and thereby revealed the mind of the Creator. The goal of his organization of the animal kingdom, Owen wrote in *The Anatomy of Vertebrates* in 1866, was to guide readers to "apprehending the unity which underlies the diversity of animal structures; to show in these structures the evidence of a predetermining Will, producing them in reference to a final purpose; and to indicate the direction and degrees in which organization, in subverting such will, rises from the general to the particular."[47] Darwin himself accepted the view that animals were designed according to a few basic blueprints, but unlike Owen saw the development of species in material and historical, not metaphysical, terms—a matter of actual genealogies and bloodlines rather than "a predetermining Will" or "ordained, continuous becoming."[48]

Owen's ideas must have been particularly congenial to Dresser. His notion of continuous creation, the idea that God invented not so much permanent species as permanent "archetypes" or "predetermined patterns" that were subsequently embodied in a variety of plant and animal forms, is a metaphysical expression of the very industrial process that many Victorian manufacturers—and Dresser himself—championed: the mass production and widespread distribution of commodities devised according to an original handmade or machine-tooled template.[49] In his great illustrated treatise *On the Nature of Limbs*, Owen sought to explain what Darwin later described as a conundrum: "that the hand of a man, formed for grasping, that of a mole for digging, the leg of a horse, the paddle of the porpoise, and the wing of a bat, should all be constructed on the same pattern."[50] Of course Darwin's solution to the puzzle lay in the idea that present-day homologies are simply morphological vestiges of old adaptations, passed down through the ages. As individuals and species were selected by nature for survival, the form of limbs—constrained by unknown laws of growth—gradually changed until they achieved present-day diversity. Owen, however, proposed that "general anatomical science reveals the unity which pervades the diversity, and demonstrates the whole skeleton of man to be the harmonized sum of a series of essentially similar segments, although each segment differs from the other, and all vary from their archetype."[51] The archetype in this case was the single vertebra, a composite form that was capable, Owen believed, of myriad and profound modification. His published drawing of the "Ideal Typical Vertebra" (Fig. 18) conveys both its archetypal and its industrial character; out of this unity, a great variety of skeletal forms may be manufactured. Resembling Dresser's flower cross-section drawings (Fig. 19) and his various abstracted plant forms in *Principles of Decorative Design*, it is notable for its perfect bilateral symmetry. A shared symmetry, Owen believed, was additional evidence of the "unity of type" of different organisms, and Dresser's almost constant use of symmetrical patterns may derive from Owen as well as from the English botanist John Lindley, whose lectures on the "Symmetry of Vegetation" in 1852 at the School of Design at Marlborough House were attended by Dresser.[52] That symmetry was put to use in the botanical sheet designed by Dresser for Jones's *Grammar of Ornament* (Fig. 20).

Semper had embraced similar views concerning types, or underlying patterns in nature, presenting them in 1853 in a lecture about Cuvier delivered at the School of Design (renamed the Department of Practical Art) when Dresser was a student there:

...when I observed this variety of nature in its simplicity, I very often thought by myself that it may be possible to reduce the creations of man, and especially the works of architecture, to certain normal and elementary forms, which, in a comparing method of contemplating them analogous to that of Cuvier for natural history, will enable us to find out the elementary forms and the principles, of which all [of the] million appearances in art are but much different modifications."[53]

The title of Dresser's 1859 book, *Unity in Variety,* both expresses the typological thinking found in Owen's *On the Nature of Limbs* and *Anatomy of Vertebrates* and in Semper's address and obviously alludes to the tradition of natural theology and Reverend Paley, who titled one of his chapters in *Natural Theology* "Of the Unity of the Deity." Indeed the preface to *Unity in Variety* explicitly praises intelligent design, and it must be seen—in the context of its appearance a few months after the publication of *The Origin of Species*—as a pointed rebuke of Darwin and Wallace:

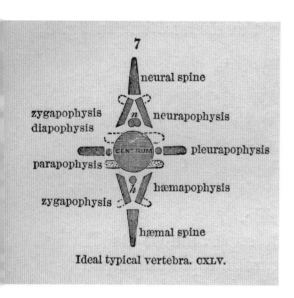

Ideal typical vertebra. CXLV.

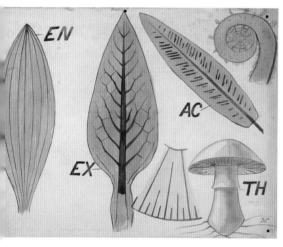

18
"Ideal Typical Vertebra"
(Fig. 7), in Richard Owen, *On the Anatomy of Vertebrates*, vol. 1, (Longmans, Green, and Co., 1866). Northwestern University Library.

19
Christopher Dresser, "Drawing from a Pedagogical Album," 1854–56, watercolor and ink on paper. Victoria and Albert Museum, London, 3958.

20
Christopher Dresser, "Various Flowers in Plan and Elevation," in Owen Jones, *The Grammar of Ornament* (London: Day and Son, 1856). Charles Deering McCormick Library of Special Collections, Northwestern University Library.

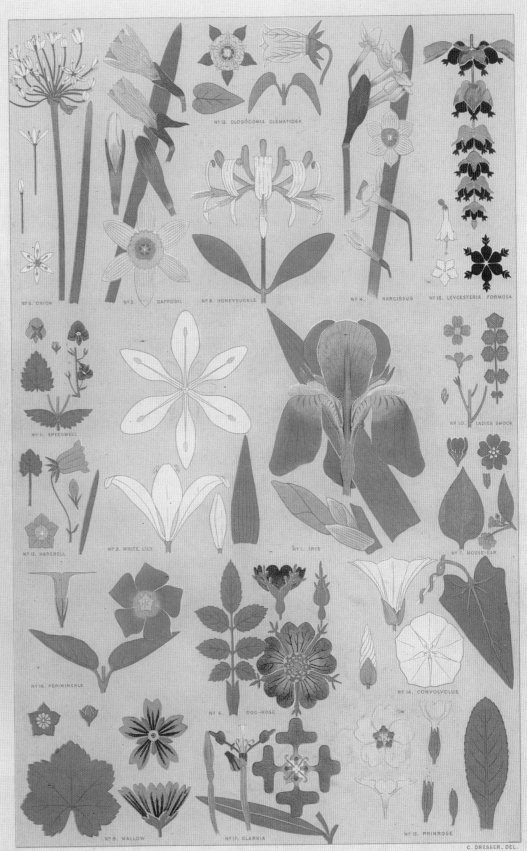

21

"The Grass of the Field," illustration in John Ruskin, *The Two Paths* (London: Smith, Elder and Co., 1859). Charles Deering McCormick Library of Special Collections, Northwestern University Library.

The consideration of the view of the vegetable kingdom contemplated in the present work are [sic] of value in another point of view; for while we trace a unity amidst all the works of creation, the mind, by an effort of its own, informs us that *one* system resulted from *one* intelligence, and thus the heart is led up from the manifold works of the beauteous creation to the one God who rules over all.[54]

And a little more than a year later, at the end of his essay on "Stem and Leaf" in the *Register of Facts and Occurrences*, Dresser wrote: "It is indeed wonderful to consider that out of a leaf and a stem the Divine Architect of the universe has fashioned all the plants that grow on the earth."[55] Compare Dresser's words to those of Bishop Wilberforce, who concluded his review of *The Origin of Species* in the *Quarterly Review* by writing that "all creation is the transcript in matter of ideas eternally existing in the mind of the Most High—that order in the utmost perfectness of its relation pervades His works, because it exists as in its centre and highest fountain-head in Him the Lord of all."[56] Compare them, too, to Digby Wyatt's words from "An Attempt to define the principles which should determine Form in the Decorative Arts," the essay cited earlier and published in 1852 in the aftermath of the Crystal Palace exhibition. He wrote: "It is impossible to examine the smallest object upon which the skill of Divinity has been exercised—a shell, a flower, or an insect— without feeling a longing to know somewhat of the mysterious laws which make that individual specimen of design so perfect, and without experiencing a desire to emulate the marvelous powers of creation."[57]

Dresser barely wavered either from his theological conception of the unity that underlies the variety of nature or his corresponding idea that the finest design required knowledge of the archetypal plant form—what Goethe, extensively cited by Dresser in his "Stem and Leaf" essay, had called the *Urpflanze*—upon which all variation is based. It was the task of the designer, Dresser believed, to patiently observe individual specimens of nature, formulate a mental image of the perfect Linnean type of which it is an example, transcribe this ideal form onto paper, adapt its morphology to the shape and function of the consumer object for which it was intended—for example, a teapot or a candle holder (see plates 10 and 15)—and then put it into production. The actual process of manufacture, Dresser believed, should be as straightforward as possible, demanding no special imagination, skill, or initiative on the part of the workman; all that was necessary was hard, routine work. Like Charles Knight and Samuel Smiles, popular author of *Self-Help* (1859), Dresser was a firm believer in industrial discipline, hierarchy, mechanization, and the salutary effects of hard work: "Labour," he wrote in *Principles of Decorative Design*, "is the means whereby we raise ourselves above our fellows; [it] is the means by which we arrive at affluence…. Workmen! I am a worker, and a believer in the efficacy of work."[58]

The contrast between Dresser's Whig, or liberal, perspective and the radicalism of Morris or even Ruskin could not be clearer. In *The Two Paths* Ruskin wrote that while great art was always about "observation of facts," it was also concerned with the "manifestation of human design and authority in the way the facts are told."[59] Both principles are displayed in Ruskin's drawing of the sinuous blades, leaves, and tendrils of *The Grass of the Field* (Fig. 21), engraved in *The Two Paths*. And he adds, in criticism of the new emphasis on rationalized design and manufacture taught at the Department of Practical Art, "The substitution of obedience to mathematical law for sympathy with observed life, is the first characteristic of the hopeless work of all ages."[60] Compare this viewpoint to one of Dresser's on plant morphology and symmetry in the *Popular Manual of Botany*, published just a year later: "The greater number of highly organized plants consist of a central rod, together with certain members which have been generated by it. All regular branchings of the central rod of the plant take place at fixed or determinate points, which later have an orderly arrangement."[61]

In *The Two Paths* Ruskin sought to prove his conviction concerning the necessary irregularity of both nature and art. He reported that "a friend"—Christopher Dresser, in all likelihood— argued that "the essence of ornament consisted in three things: contrast, series, and symmetry."[62] Ruskin challenged the assertion by mailing him an inkblot, which represented contrast; the numbers 1 through 6, which stood for series; and a crude stick figure, which stood for symmetry (Fig. 22). None of these, Ruskin said, could be considered valid ornament. The unnamed designer, however, was undaunted: "Your materials," he wrote, "were not ornament, because you did not

apply them," and included with his post a pattern for "a sporting neckerchief" (Fig. 23) made up of all these forms, organized according to rules of symmetry, contrast, and series. Ruskin, however, was not persuaded by the clever demonstration and claimed that the key design decisions were not the consequence of the application of rule but the result of his interlocutor's sophisticated "sense and judgment...skill and taste." For Ruskin, as for Morris later on, symmetry, order, and typology could not be substituted for craft, skill, imagination, and even caprice.

But from what I have so far argued, it should not be concluded that Dresser was wholly impervious to evolutionism or even to Darwinian natural selection. In *The Art of Decorative Design* (1862) and later works, Dresser's very design stringency, rejected by Ruskin and Morris, exposes a highly rationalist approach to decoration and design, whereby particular materials are judged only to be suited to specific functions and certain designs are deemed appropriate only for certain corresponding forms. Derived, as we have seen, from classical notions of decorum and 18th- and 19th-century theories of propriety, the functionalist argument had received its clearest modern articulation in Pugin, but was given a decidedly evolutionary slant by Dresser. He argued that it was imperative that artists devise no objects that exceeded the requirement of function and need; otherwise the items in question would violate the laws of nature and good design. In a Darwinian vein, he concludes: "[For] we must select those objects that are best adapted to the circumstances in which they are to be placed."[63] A decade later, in *Principles of Decorative Design,* Dresser would write: "I might multiply illustrations of this principle of fitness, or adaptation to purpose, as manifested in plants, to an almost indefinite extent; but when all had been said we should yet have the simple truth before us, that the chief end which we should have in creating any object, is that of rendering it perfectly fitted to the proposed end."[64]

In so insisting on "fitness" or "adaptation to purpose" as the goal of all design, Dresser was placing himself in the camp of the evolutionary anthropologists who likewise argued that the history of the material or industrial arts (whether among so-called savage or civilized races) was one of constant development. In *Primitive Culture* (1871) the Oxford ethnologist Tylor stated that "the early development of arts [may be traced] not to a blind instinct, but to a selection, imitation, and gradual adaptation and improvement of objects and operations which Nature, the instructor of primeval man, set before him." Tylor then listed tool after tool, weapon after weapon, and artifact after artifact that had resulted from the slow and steady evolution toward greater functionality:

hatchet into battle-axe, javelin into bow and arrow, club into boomerang, rattles and drums into pipes and stringed instruments. "So with architecture and agriculture," Tylor adds, "Complex, elaborate, and highly reasoned as are the upper stages of these arts, it is to be remembered that their lower stages begin with mere direct imitation of nature, copying the shelters which nature provides and the propagation of plants which nature performs."[65]

Dresser's practice as a designer and theorist reveals that he accepted some aspects of evolutionism and even Darwinism in the artistic and manufacturing sphere—in particular the idea of selection based on adaptation—but largely denied it in biology. There, he believed, natural theology and the typological systems of Cuvier, Goethe, Owen, and Semper still held sway. "Plants are founded upon a geometrical basis," Dresser wrote, and "the most worthy ornaments have a like basis, and as order most clearly manifests the operation of mind, we deduce that order is essential to the production of exalted ornament."[66] This approach resulted in an artistic style and procedure that, for all its ingenuity and originality, was often awkward in form and contradictory in feeling. The supremely subtle and highly rationalist rhetoric apparent in his large *Watering Can* (see plate 13) and *Teapot* (see plate 10) was gainsaid by a whimsical, bizarre, and even grotesque manner visible elsewhere—for example, in his *Goat Vase* (see plate 6) and *Tongue Vase* (see plate 7). This very division, however, reveals Dresser's modernity: The surface decoration or sculptural ornamentation often appears so ostentatious that the viewer is compelled to consider the possibility of its opposite—an ornament-free design, which of course Dresser also provided, especially with his work in silver. Dresser himself understood the implications of his own procedure, sometimes creating objects of stunning abstract clarity, such as the diamond-shaped silver teapot in the collection of the Victoria and Albert Museum, the rectilinear copper and brass tea kettle and the teapot and creamer (see plates 11 and 12). This was precisely the outcome most feared by Ruskin and Morris, who struggled valiantly to maintain a role for individual craftsmanship and intuitive design in the teeth of a manufacturing system that favored standardization—the mass production of inexpensive functional objects by use and reuse of a die, pattern, or archetype.

Dresser's modernity was of course more apparent than real; the simplicity, abstraction, and archetypal character of his work is ultimately derived not from the conditions and circumstances of modern life, nor from a desired truth to materials, but from adherence to a vision of nature and design derived from Paley, natural theology, Goethe, and archetypal thinking. His great works in metal, ceramic, and glass are not so much anticipations of Bauhaus design as radically reactionary manifestations of an older, indeed increasingly vestigial worldview. Yet a comparison of Dresser's work with that of modern designers who largely rejected ornament—from Adolf Loos to Marianne Brandt—is nevertheless apt. For it was Dresser, in anticipation of 20th-century developments, who embraced a rationalized design and production process for the purpose of making his merchandise more widely available and affordable. And it was Dresser, in anticipation of the utopian worldview of the Bauhaus artists and planners, who largely rejected contingency and change as a basis for design in the faith that he had devised objects and forms that stood outside of history.

Coda: Design after Darwin—Sullivan, Wright, Voysey, and Ashbee

Opposites sometimes meet: Ultimately as inescapable for Dresser as for Morris, evolutionism and adaptation structured the works of both men. Both were "pioneers," as Nikolaus Pevsner put it, of a modern design that stressed the union of form and function—in the one case because of obedience to the principle that the perfect adaptation of design to use was a testimonial to the logic, perfection, and unity of God and nature; and in the other because of a moral and political imperative to abolish repetitive, mind-numbing labor and to create a domestic environment in which waste, excess, and an alienating luxury were eliminated. And Dresser and Morris are linked in another way: By the end of the 19th century, each man's political and design stance was used to sanction its perfect antithesis; through the cunning of history, each—though deeply suspicious of many aspects of modernization and rationalization—became an instrument of that very progress.

Dresser's idealist art, conservative ideas, and notion of the divinely inspired archetype paved the way for Art Nouveau, the Werkbund, Bauhaus, and subsequent modernist architectural forms, each of which embraced secular, materialist, scientific, and collective approaches to labor, design, and manufacture. In addition, his principle "of *fitness, or adaptation to purpose*, as manifested in plants" was a basis for the organic design of Louis Sullivan and Frank Lloyd Wright (as David Van Zanten discusses here) each of whom projected democratic and communal social visions at variance with the liberal, individualist, bootstrap entrepreneurialism promoted by Dresser. Though Sullivan and Wright were influenced by a great variety of intellectual and design sources, they also looked closely at the designs of Jones and Dresser.

Sullivan had been exposed to Dresser during his residence and brief period of training in the early 1870s in Philadelphia with the architect Frank Furness. There he gained an understanding of the process of abstracting and stylizing natural forms based on their presumed underlying structural principles, as is apparent in ornaments he made in Chicago in the 1870s for Moody's Tabernacle and the Sinai Synagogue, and in the 1880s for the Scoville Building (see plate 48) and the Wineman Residence (see plate 61). Almost 20 years later, in 1893, this abstraction—which Sullivan called "the Universal Law" of rhythm—is even more apparent in the *Elevator Grille* (see plate 56) for the Chicago Stock Exchange.[67] Here natural forms are reduced to mere ciphers, articulating a syncopation that anticipates the language of jazz, to be invented in New Orleans and Chicago a decade or so later.

Wright also absorbed the lessons of Dresser in his consistent emphasis on stylization, typology, machine production, and, of course, "the organic," the latter being one of the architect's favorite words. The decorative results of the approach are apparent, for example, in the slender copper *Weed Holder* (see plate 64) made to his specifications by James A. Miller and Brothers around 1900, the bulbous *Urn* (see plate 65), and his cast concrete architectural decorations. But here Wright blended idealist doctrines concerning *Urformen*, with an evolutionism that is Darwinian in it emphasis on organicism, adaptation, and fitness of form to function. In an important 1908 essay "In the Cause of Architecture," he wrote:

I do not believe we will ever again have the uniformity of type which has characterized the so-called great styles. Conditions have changed; our ideal is Democracy, the highest possible expression of the individual as a unit not inconsistent with the harmonious whole. The average of human intelligence rises steadily, and as the individual unit grows more and more to be trusted we will have an architecture with richer *variety in unity* than has ever arisen before; but the forms must be born out of our changed conditions.[68] [author's emphasis]

Wright's words reflect the diversity of his intellectual debts—Ralph Waldo Emerson, Walt Whitman, and Herbert Spencer come to mind. But his phrase "variety in unity" is undoubtedly a purposeful inversion of the key concept derived from, among others, William Paley, Richard Owen, and especially Christopher Dresser: "unity in variety." For Dresser, the apparent multiplicity of individual specimens, and indeed the whole natural world, belies a oneness derived from the genius of the mind of God, the great designer; for Wright, the social and political unity, or "harmonious whole," of modern democratic life is the precondition for an individuality and variety previously unimagined.

Wright's sentiment is also indebted, in all likelihood, to Oscar Wilde. In "The Soul of Man under Socialism" (1891), the aesthete argued that though a few creative men and women at present use the freedom purchased by their wealth to produce things of great beauty and subtlety that express their individuality, the mass of humanity has its souls and creativity crushed by oppressive labor that it must perform simply to survive.[69] That dichotomy, which underlay the Morris-Dresser debate, would be ended, Wilde believed, by a new regime of voluntary association and socialism. Wright argued that a new industrial and political order, organized beneath the banners of Democracy, Individuality, Organicism, and Variety in Unity, would make possible a new architecture and design perfectly adapted to the needs of modern citizens.

Morris's materialist and contingent approach to form and design, derived from the acute observation of nature, Gothic architecture, and other premodern or so-called Barbaric styles, would, in spite of his intentions, become a basis for modernization and an architectural rhetoric of British gentrification. Voysey, who is discussed at greater length elsewhere in this book, is perhaps the most achieved architect (along with Philip Webb) associated with the Arts and Crafts

movement. But he in fact embraced a kind of typological design closer in many respects to the example of Dresser than his putative master, Morris. His wallpaper and textile patterns, such as the *Saladin* (Fig. 24) and the *Tokio* (see plate 32), with their unmasked repeats and their highly stylized, even streamlined plant and animal forms, would appear to be ideally suited for the suburban and rural homes of a generation of wealthy and powerful modernizing English industrialists, financiers, and entrepreneurs. Though rejecting what he considered mindless labor, he embraced the simple shapes and forms that may be stamped out by machine production:

When you design my tables and chairs, you will think of the machine that is going to help in the making, and choose such shapes as are easily worked by machinery. When labour was cheap and men uneducated and less fit for more intellectual work, the legs and arms of tables and chairs were charmingly curved and formed by hand into fanciful shapes, and delight us still with their human subtlety. But now, alas! Your wood comes to you machine-sawn and machine-planed, and the only thoughts and feeling you can put into your furniture must be through a mechanical medium. So right proportions and the natural qualities of the wood, the suitable color and texture of the upholstery make up your limited vocabulary.[70]

For Voysey, adaptation of Arts and Crafts ideals to modern conditions of manufacture, labor organization, and capital was the highest ideal of the modern architect and designer.

Ashbee, too, as discussed further in this book, began as a craftsman and socialist in the tradition of Ruskin and Morris. He also celebrated contingency as a fact that governed both nature and handcraft, rejecting the typological approach of Dresser. Especially in his silverwork, which often eschewed the smooth, polished surfaces of most fine English metalwork (including Dresser's) from the previous two centuries, is concerned with history, intuition, and the transformation of the vernacular into the refined and even the sublime. His *Dish with Double Loop Handles* (see plate 44) and his elegant gilded copper *Chalice* (or sporting cup) (see plate 42), reminiscent of work by the Italian Renaissance master Benvenuto Cellini, alike reveal the blows of the planishing hammer and thus the physical labor of the metalworker. In addition, the attenuation of the handles of the one and the elongation of the stem of the other suggest vitality and progress. It is almost as if the craftsman had arrested the development of the vessels at a single moment in time, but that they might resume their growth at any moment.

The succession of craft workshops and labor communes Ashbee established—first in East London in 1888, then in Chipping Campden in the Cotswolds—put into practice socialist principles of cooperation only suggested by Morris. In the beginning at least, every worker in the Guild of Handicraft was a shareholder. Like Voysey, Ashbee gradually came to embrace modern technology and industry as the inevitable adaptation of productive methods to the conditions of modern life. His social and political views, generally in line with what is called Guild Socialism, promoted the idea that workshop or factory self-management was the means whereby labor exploitation could be ended and the basis established for a genuine egalitarian democracy. But he also apparently embraced aspects of Spencerian evolutionism, especially the idea that power or "force" was the "ultimate of ultimates" that underlay nature, and that the physical world and human society alike were in a constant state of striving, development, and growth toward betterment.[71] These ideas, widespread at the end of the century, are implicit in Ashbee's praise of Sullivan in a lecture he delivered in Chicago in 1901. Descending one of the city's "steel towers," Ashbee walked along the street at twilight and wrote:

I found myself by some strangeness of fancy opposite a gate of Mr. Sullivan's, a wonderful bronze gate it was, full of the romance of architecture. You saw stars when you looked at it, like you saw when someone hit you between the eyes and you appreciate the vigour of the blow. The forms in it were nervous, electric, restless, but through all was a sentiment of growth.... [Soon] everything opened out as with great light, nervous white light, and there was sound of swift, unintelligible movement, of power that was rhythmic, only the sense was not yet born to understand.[72]

Had Ashbee already read Wright's 1901 Hull House address, "The Art and Craft of the Machine," with its stirring encomia to energy, industry, a mechanized craft workshop, and the "pulse of activity in this great city"?[73] Ashbee had met Wright in 1896, had been to Hull House, and would host Wright in Chipping Campden in the Cotswolds in 1901. By 1917, Ashbee's Spencerianism was undisguised:

The doctrine of Evolution has now become part of our thought. No aesthetic philosophy is conceivable without it. We realize now the 'ascent of man towards truth, goodness and beauty.'... We know now that if we practice an art that is no longer in and of our own time, that Art is of little consequence.... Here [in the United States] in the hands of Frank Lloyd Wright the processes of standardization...have been so perfected that it is possible for one creative mind to build with an almost infinite variety of mechanical parts, each of which has been in the first instance thought out in reference to the machine that has made it or that will finally put it into its place on the building. There is no limit to the variations that one imaginative mind can give to houses thus set together, and I conceive that many beautiful cities are likely to grow up by these methods.[74]

For Ashbee, as for Voysey, Wright, and Sullivan, evolutionism—tinged with a Spencerian faith in infinite progress—was the framework for the new marriage of form and function and the adaptation of design to the new modern circumstances of economic and social life. Though clearly influenced by the archetypes of Dresser, these designers and architects nevertheless rejected any transcendent basis for design, and came to believe that industrialization and mechanization were the instrument whereby, in Darwin's words, "endless forms most beautiful and most wonderful have been, and are being evolved."

Louis Sullivan, Herbert Spencer, and the Medium of Architecture

David Van Zanten

I

"It is...difficult to learn from Mr. Sullivan just what he has done. He refers to the work you will see about the stage opening as the differentiation of an absolute truth and something having to do with Spencer's first principles and Darwin's doctrine of evolution, with the predicate of a flower and an ordinary staircase for an hypothesis."

—*Chicago Daily Inter-Ocean*, August 12, 1882 (on Sullivan's decoration of Hooley's Theatre)

Louis Sullivan's voluminous writings have always been subsumed in organicist, evolutionary thought.[1] He himself cited Charles Darwin, Herbert Spencer, and Hippolyte Taine; he wrote an admiring letter to Walt Whitman in 1887; he could not have escaped knowledge of John Ruskin; he had links to Eugène Emmanuel Viollet-le-Duc.[2] In the quotation that heads this essay—his first recorded general declaration about design, made when he was 25—Sullivan was clearly trying to communicate what he made of Herbert Spencer's *First Principles* (1862)—namely, Spencer's distinction between systems of static truth ("ultimate truth," in Spencer's words) and his own notion of endless reciprocal adaptation and evolution. (Darwin's importance for Sullivan, on the other hand, appears to have been less direct, paralleling that which he had for Spencer: He offered scientific proof of this endless change in nature.[3]) *First Principles* is pointedly and laboriously constructed, the body of the book being a series of chapters explaining progressively the instability in nature and humankind, dominated by forces that transform but never dissipate matter, energy, and society. Chapters are titled "The Indestructibility of Matter," "The Continuity of Motion," "The Persistence of Force," "The Persistence of Relations among Forces," "The Transformation and Equivalence of Forces," "The Direction of Motion," "The Rhythm of Motion," etc. Every force engenders a counterforce; each step in evolution engenders a countervailing step towards dissolution, all in eternal negotiation. His chapter "Rhythm in Motion," for example, takes off from the movement of a becalmed ship's pennant shaking itself in a starting wind, passes through the rhythmic pulse of the billowing full sail, on to the spiraling of astronomical nebulae and the fidgeting courses of water currents and the river traces they impose. From here Spencer moves to plants, animals, and human societies constantly adjusting themselves to changing natural and social competition—compressing in a dozen pages an amazing mass of parallel examples with huge jumps in kind and scale.

This is the text, then, Sullivan cites to explain large constructed floral motifs of the sort we see in a design for the Wineman residence and a chimney panel for the Rubel residence (see plates 61 and 49), which evidently he had abstracted step by step from natural prototypes in the manner of the French master of floral ornamentation, Victor Marie Ruprich-Robert, whose drawings (Fig. 1) Sullivan had copied.[4] I cite Ruprich-Robert's plates not just because Sullivan knew them but also because Sullivan—Genevois on his maternal side and competent in French—had studied first under the French designer Eugène Létang at the Massachusetts Institute of Technology (1872–73), then in Létang's old atelier, that of Emile Vaudremer, at the Ecole des Beaux-Arts in Paris (1874–75) when he lived across the street from the Ecole des Arts Décoratifs where Ruprich-Robert was teaching the course on ornamental composition. Ruprich-Robert had succeeded Viollet-le-Duc there and elaborated his ideas as a pedagogical system.[5] Sullivan's future collaborator in Chicago,

Louis Sullivan, *Elevator Door* (detail of plate 55), Chicago Stock Exchange Building, 1894, bronze. Collection of John Vinci; courtesy of Richard Nickel Committee, Chicago.

1

V. Ruprich-Robert, Plate 108
from *Flore Ornementale.*
*Essai sur la composition de
l'ornement* (Paris: Dunod,
1876). Private Collection.

AJUSTEMENT.

Louis Millet (son of a close friend of Viollet-le-Duc), had started his training at the Ecole des Arts Décoratifs, in 1873 under the direction of his uncle, sculptor Aimé Millet, who was an instructor there, and Vaudremer's collaborator Eugène Train, who continued as his master when he studied at the Ecole des Beaux-Art from 1874 to 1879. In May 1875 Sullivan returned to Chicago and entered into a short-lived partnership with John Edelmann, designing extravagant floral efflorescences to decorate the interiors of the Moody Tabernacle and the Sinai Synagogue. (Edelmann was a proselytizing anarchist and, in 1897, having moved to New York, Prince Kropotkin's American host.[6]) After moving from office to office, in 1881 Sullivan became, through Edelmann's intermediacy, junior designing partner for the established German-born engineer Dankmar Adler, and what soon became one of the great theater and skyscraper firms of the country coalesced around them (until its dissolution in 1895) with the engineer Paul Mueller and the draftsmen Frank Lloyd Wright, Irving Gill, and George Elmslie. Then, around 1900, as work dried up, Sullivan retreated into a strange Melville-like withdrawal focused on writing and drawing.

Sullivan's organicist, evolutionary thinking was made more systematically and artfully manifest in his 1886 prose poem "Inspiration," which he had read to the startled members of the Western Association of Architects in 1886, sent to Walt Whitman in 1887, hoping for comment, and edited and translated into French before a trip to Paris in 1893.[7] This was a lengthy evocation of the seasons in nature, transmuting Spencer's *First Principles* into poetry. Sullivan's prose poem is simple in structure—its sections are titled "Growth—a Spring Song," "Decadence—Autumn Reverie," "The Infinite—a Song of the Depths"—and clear in its stated intent: It suggests that artistic evolution in its character and quality reproduces this cycling in nature. It is especially interesting to follow its construction, its interweaving of images of the seasons, times of day, periods of life, elements of nature (cloudscapes, sunsets, forests, seas). Sullivan ends mixing all this:

In tranquility of meditation the soul unites with nature as raindrops unite with the sea; whence are exhaled vapors, under the hot and splendid sun of inspired imagination, vapors rising through the atmosphere of high endeavor to drift away in beauteous clouds, borne upon the imponderable winds of purpose, to condense and descend at last as tangible realities…. Whence the dominant, all-pervading thought that a spontaneous and vital art must come fresh from nature, and can only thus come…. That such a dawning is close upon this land there can be no longer be any doubt. In the paling gloom the phantoms flit about, uneasy and restless, loosing identity. The heavens are faint with the flow of a new desire; and with overflowing heart I rise through the mists, aloft, to catch a glimpse of the coming sun, and carol this prophetic song of spring.

The culmination of Sullivan's writing was his *Autobiography of an Idea,* published just before his death in 1924, together with his parallel graphic *A System of Architectural Ornament.* The latter ends with 11 sheets of pure, scaleless ornamental fantasy, paralleling, in the rise and fall of their elaboration, Sullivan's own artistic life and reprising his depiction of cyclical nature in "Inspiration," coincident with Spencer's evocation of eternal aggregation and dissolution in his *First Principles*.

II

---

*The Sullivanian philosophy, so far as it was personal to him, is written in that chosen language
[of pencil-drawn ornament] most clearly and if you are going to read* him *at all, it is there to be read
at level best…He was miraculous when he drew.*

—Frank Lloyd Wright, *Genius and the Mobocracy,* 1949

It is not Sullivan's writing, however, that I want to explore here, but his drawings in the light of these writings, as Frank Lloyd Wright admonishes above.

Sullivan worked through drawings, extraordinary ornamental drawings—in poverty at the end of his career he could do nothing else—like the 24 by 30 inch sheets of his *System of Architectural Ornament.*[8] But at the busy height of his career he made them in order to work out exact effects, as in the Pueblo Grand Opera House cross section in the exhibition (plate 62) or the Auditorium banquet hall capital studies he gave to Wright just before his death.[9] In his obituary appreciation, Wright himself depicted the moment of germination of the Wainwright Building facade as evident in a (lost) sketch: "When he brought in the board with the motive of the Wainwright Building outlined in profile and in scheme upon it and threw it on my table, I was perfectly aware of what had happened. This was Louis Sullivan's greatest moment—his greatest effort. The 'skyscraper,' as a new thing beneath the sun, an entity with virtue, individuality and beauty all its own, was born."[10] He continued: "Ah, that supreme, erotic high adventure of the mind that was his ornament! Often I would see him, his back bent over his drawing board, intent upon what?… Beside this sensuous master of adventure with tenuous, vibrant, plastic form, Casanova was a duffer, Gil Blas a torn chapeau;…The soul of Rabelais could have understood and would have called him brother." In *Genius and the Mobocracy,* Wright continued this thought as quoted at the beginning of this section.

What is important about Sullivan's submergence in drawing is this: The cult of work, of thoughtful fabrication, that drove the organicist ethics expounded in various ways by Ruskin, Viollet-le-Duc, or Whitman arrived among architects just when they were being drawn away from close contact with building. A corps of obedient, trained intermediaries coalesced during the late 19th century, including draftsmen like Wright and Elmslie, decorators like Millet, fabricators like Kristian Schneider, engineers like Dankmar Adler and Paul Mueller, general contractors like George

A. Fuller.[11] Buildings became big and complicated, skyscrapers not the least among them. The architect was gathered into the managerial class and alienated from his work. By 1881 and the founding of Sullivan's partnership with Adler, the architect's labor was done at a distance through drawings. It is clearly then naive to think, as Ruskin and Morris had, that much morally was accomplished by setting the workmen to discovering nature and patiently expressing themselves in wood, stone, and iron—as in the case of the O'Shea brothers working for Ruskin at the Oxford University Museum (1858) until they were fired for caricaturing the authorities, or the carvers employed on Peter B. Wight's National Academy of Design in New York (1865) who, we are told, returned gratefully afterward to cutting familiar conventional capitals and moldings as soon as they were done. Martin Nadaud, the mid-century stonecutter cum autobiographer cum political activist, makes it clear that morality for him was achieving minimally sufficient living and working conditions. What he admired in the stonecutting was doing the thing neatly, with physical effort minimized, as demonstrated by his friend Maffrand, "*un des meilleurs maçons de Paris.*"[12] The riveting images of work Ruskin has left us in his carpet-like watercolors of building facades and surfaces in Verona and Venice are as powerful because of the labor on his part as they are records of the work of time in their weathering and dilapidation and their documentation of the original effort of the medieval craftsmen who produced them. The direct projection of organicist principles onto a building through the work of its construction was a Victorian delusion. What was left to the architect was drawing, and, as Wright emphasized, Sullivan truly understood its power and morality.

In her forthcoming book Lauren Weingarden proposes that Sullivan worked metaphorically. By close analysis of his designs around 1890 in relation to Whitman, to Impressionist painting, and to the broader Ruskinian tradition, she argues three points: that Sullivan believed architecture could achieve effects of poetry and painting,[13] that it could thus represent the vital forces of the natural landscape in their transient effects as the means of evoking poetic experiences, and finally that this discourse brought out Sullivan's debt to the Emersonian/Whitmanesque tradition of the "poet-revelator," from whose study of nature a new American art might develop. That is to say, Weingarden argues, that Sullivan's ornament was not just an emanation of structural surfaces but their transformation, that it was laid over them like a veil through which an experience of light and life—a sort of flicker—might be inspired, as in, for example, the colored webs covering the surfaces of his Stock Exchange Trading Room, evoking a summer forest.[14] That is to say, Sullivan saw his architecture as sensory manipulation, and his medium was ornamental overlay.

2
Louis Sullivan, *Ground Floor Plan, Joseph & Harold C. Bradley Residence*, Madison, Wisconsin, 1908. William Gray Purcell Papers, Northwest Architectural Archives, University of Minnesota Libraries.

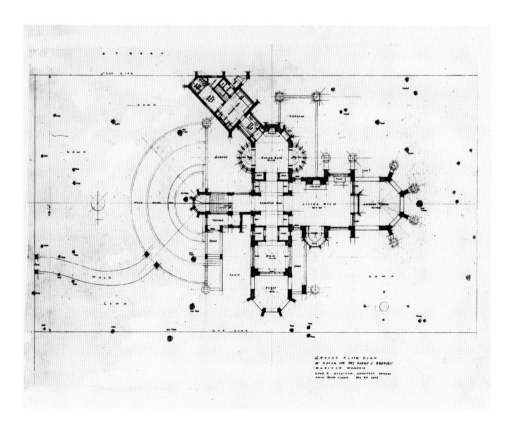

PLATE 13

3
Louis Sullivan, Plate 13 from
*A System of Architectural
Ornament According with a
Philosophy of Man's Powers*
(New York: Press of the Amer-
ican Institute of Architects,
1924). Charles Deering
McCormick Library of Special
Collections, Northwestern
University Library.

4
Delineator unknown,
*Business Center from Plan
of Chicago*, 1909. Chicago
History Museum.

I would argue, by extension, that Sullivan's enterprise was indeed metaphorical, but it was so within its representation: The labor of Sullivan's drawing was a metaphor for Ruskin's and Nadaud's shifting of stones. His ornament, though floral in motif, is essentially abstract so that it could respond subtly to its situation. In my book *Sullivan's City* I have argued that it is thus scale-less and that we see Sullivan applying the same generative moves in producing a house plan like that of the Bradley residence dated December 24, 1908 (Fig. 2), or a sheet of ornament like those of his *System of Architectural Ornament*. Among its sheets is at least one plate, number 13, that in its elaborateness and changes across its surface evokes a city plan—all the more tellingly because in general layout the specific city it suggests is Chicago in Daniel Burnham's plan of 1909, and specifi-cally its projection of the Loop (Figs. 3 and 4). What, aside from complexity, defines Sullivan's sheet as ornament and Burnham's draftsman's as a city plan? On the one hand, nothing: Each is a pat-tern generated from a central point so that major and minor elements fall into their proper place, decoratively in the case of Sullivan's plan, institutionally in the case of Burnham's. On the other hand, everything: The Burnham plan firmly establishes a continuous ground plane in front of which projects a uniform plateau of 10-story building tops and behind which spreads a placid lake/river datum. Sullivan's drawing weaves back and forth between a dozen planes with a grid of graphic peaks and chasms. Burnham's plan maps Chicago, while Sullivan's evokes it. Burnham's plan sug-gests a static tableau down its main axis and out to the lake; Sullivan's sheet encourages an active exploration of paths and byways, drawing one's eye through its labyrinth. It is Sullivan's city, in its density and variety, that is more faithful to Chicago's futuristic city center as, for example, Wright described it at the end of his famous 1901 essay, "The Art and Craft of the Machine":

How the voice of this monstrous thing, this greatest of machines, a great city, rises to proclaim the marvel of the units of its structure, the ghastly warning boom from the deep throats of the vessels heavily seeking inlet to the waterway below, answered by the echoing clangor of the bridge bells growing nearer and more ominous as the vessel cuts momentarily the flow of the nearer artery, warning the current from the swinging bridge now closing on its stately passage, just in time to receive a rush of steam, as a streak of light, the avalanche of blood and metal hurled across it and gone, roaring into the night on its glittering bands of steel...[15]

The basic trope running through almost every chapter of Spencer's *First Principles* is the functioning of parallel structures in different contexts and at different scales. Here the transformation of these imbricated scales in Sullivan's drawing finally escapes eclecticism, since the same construction produces all the forms of building—plan and ornament, exterior shapes and interior volumes—like Russian dolls fitting endlessly together, without a gap. With eclecticism, inside spaces had been enclosed within a picturesque outside not necessarily congruent with them and characterized with the superscription of ornamental touches. Now in this Chicago grammar, interior pushes through to generate exterior—less as volumes than as continuous pattern and rhythm—while ornament is constructed like the plan, or even like the man-made gridded environment.

III

A building should be adapted to the climate of the locality in which it is built. Such a building as the Pueblo Grand Opera House would not be suited for the climate of Chicago, and we would therefore not build anything like it in Chicago. The climate of Pueblo is dry and warm, the atmosphere is glaring and the air very clear. It is noticeable, however, that no matter how great one's distress may be while in the sun, the moment one enters the shade he becomes comfortable. This, in general, will account for the style of the building and the general working out of the design is merely an elaboration of a theory that every city should have an architecture distinctly its own.

—Louis Sullivan quoted in *Pueblo Sunday Opinion*, October 5, 1890

In the above quotation Sullivan explains to another newspaper reporter what he was trying to achieve in the Grand Opera House in Pueblo, Colorado, designed almost a decade after Hooley's Theatre, in 1888–90.[16] I want to take this as indicating a crisis in design, implicit in the structure's rugged, impressionistic Neo-Romanesque exterior, which extended that of Sullivan's Auditorium (1886–90) and Walker Warehouse (1888–89), both in Chicago, as well as his first round-arched project for the Wainwright Building in Saint Louis, published in the *Globe Democrat* of November 29, 1890.[17] Sullivan's ultimate objective at Pueblo, he explained to the reporter, was to achieve for every individual city "an architecture distinctively its own." He specified climate as the primary factor: temperature and the quality of air and light. He characterizes his reaction to these as manifest in the style of the building and in the "general working out of the design." Here, in October 1890, Sullivan was still confusing the "working out" of a design with conventions of style (as also in the first Wainwright project), but a few months later he had reshaped his Wainwright design (Fig. 5) to produce something startlingly new by a more literal process of "working out." Here Sullivan's discovery, to put it simply, was to treat the facades of this cubic 10-story office block as if they were sheets of paper. Looked at head on, each facade consists of a patterned field centered on the blank surface of the building mass. The puzzling lack of emphases at the bottom and the lateral edges explain themselves as the ground upon which this motif is inscribed. An over-scaled frieze at the top below a box-lid cornice transforms this cube into an office building. He has moved from painterly to graphic, from "impressionistic" to constructive.

This was a compositional gambit (discovering the center of his "sheet" and working his design outward) Sullivan would later demonstrate in the Bradley house plan of 1908 where he found his constructive paradigm in the elaboration of ornament.[18] The Bradley plan is the only surviving pencil design drawing showing his construction lines.[19] What these reveal is a centrifugal composition of spaces generated along two cross-axes, these axes crossed by secondary axes whose intersection gives rise to subordinate centrifugal elaborations: the smoking room in the lower part of the drawing discovered by erecting diagonals from the intersection; the dining room above whose paired bow windows effloresce from where the secondary axis crosses the facade line; the half-octagonal stair tower at the front whose center point becomes the point of rotation of a rainbow of garden beds or terraces Sullivan imagined spreading out from the house toward the street. But the most fascinating detail of Sullivan's pencil construction here is that the point of intersection of the two major axes from which the whole composition is elaborated was fixed by the extension of the centerlines of the lot itself, as if that lot was the sheet upon which the motif was generated, as I have suggested of the building mass of the Wainwright structure. A conventional architect would have worked from the outside in, drawing out the city-legislated facade and side fire set-backs, then dividing the box defined by these framing lines to accommodate the required interior spaces.

The emergence of this ornamental design technique in Sullivan's work is evident within a circle of 200 yards in Chicago's Graceland Cemetery, from Sullivan's Ryerson Tomb (1887–90) to that erected by Ryerson's business partner Henry Harrison Getty (1890–91). What in the Ryerson monument is a matter of shape, surface, color, and fabrication—minimal, sheer, and funereal black in cyclopean blocks—becomes in the Getty block a mini-Wainwright Building, the evenly patterned waist of the cube wrapped like the Wainwright window field around it above an unornamented plinth, box-lid cornice clamped on top.

The result was a peculiar indefiniteness of scale already captured by an anonymous writer for the New York *Engineering News* in December 1891 with the phrase "toy-block architecture": "Toy-Block Architecture seems the most suitable name for a species of design which appears to have originated in Chicago….It is as though a child with an assortment of toy blocks had erected such a structure [as Sullivan's Fraternity Temple] as the fancy of the moment suggested." The *Engineering News,* in fact, is citing the second step Sullivan had taken in his thinking, where, in response to the commission for a 34-story "Fraternity Temple" to cover most of a Chicago city block, he piled up a tiered series of Wainwright Buildings to produce a Babylonian solution to the admission of light to the city's streets, a conception he simultaneously embodied in a sketch in the Chicago *Graphic* envisioning a future city of such ziggurat skyscrapers, each with a distinctive characterizing pinnacle.[20]

5
Louis Sullivan, *Wainwright Building*, St. Louis, 1891 (Photograph 1983).

The winter of 1890–91 was a moment of illumination, when Sullivan discovered his retreat on the Gulf Coast, as he later wrote in his *Autobiography of an Idea*:

'Twas here that Louis did his finest, purest thinking. 'Twas here he saw the flow of life, that all life became a flowing for him, and so the thoughts the works of man. 'Twas here he saw the witchery of nature's fleeting moods—those dramas gauged in seconds. 'Twas here he gazed into the depths of that flowing, as the mystery of countless living functions moved silently from the mystery of palpable or impalpable form.... 'Twas here Louis underwent that metamorphosis that is all there is of him, that spiritual illumination which knows no why and no wherefor [sic].... Arrived in Chicago, Louis at once went to work with his old-time vim.[21]

A cascade of new designs followed—the Wainwright and Getty projects, the Schiller Building and the Transportation Pavilion for the Columbian Exposition, the Charnley House, the Fraternity Temple project, and, most especially to my mind, the 18 capital designs for the banquet hall hurriedly added to the Auditorium in spring 1891—each in a magnificently independent form playing with the "toy-block" quality of his Wainwright solution. Ultimately Sullivan's ornament would detach from its architectural surface entirely and become a screen in front of it, as in the two lower stories of the Carson Pirie Scott Store (1898–1903), or syncopate against the architectural organism, as in the Van Allen Store in Clinton, Iowa (1911–14).

I have quoted Wright in his 1924 obituary of Sullivan and his *Genius and the Mobocracy*, saying that he immediately understood the implications of the Wainwright design when thrown on his desk for elaboration—namely, "the dawn of a new day in skyscraper architecture." Wright had good reason to be so categorical, because he himself took the next step in February 1901, inventing the Prairie House in his *Ladies' Home Journal* project, "A Home in a Prairie Town," Neil Levine has argued, by a parallel decorative generation from the American agricultural grid.[22] In that publication there is a small block plan—made much more prominent when the drawings were republished in the 1902 Chicago Architectural Club catalogue—showing this first "Prairie" house replicated four times, pin-wheeling around a square Midwestern suburban block (Fig. 6). Levine argues that the rectilinear, spiraling geometry of the "Prairie" house derives, in fact, from that of this man-made

6

Frank Lloyd Wright, "Fifth design in the *Ladies' Home Journal* Series of Modern Suburban Houses," from *The Chicago Architectural Annual* (Chicago: Chicago Architectural Club, 1902). Charles Deering McCormick Library of Special Collections, Northwestern University Library.

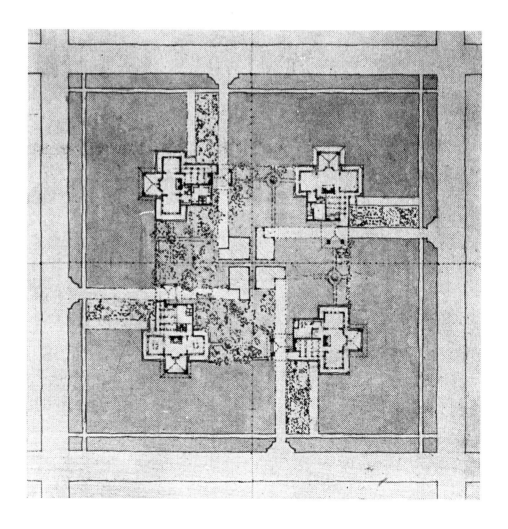

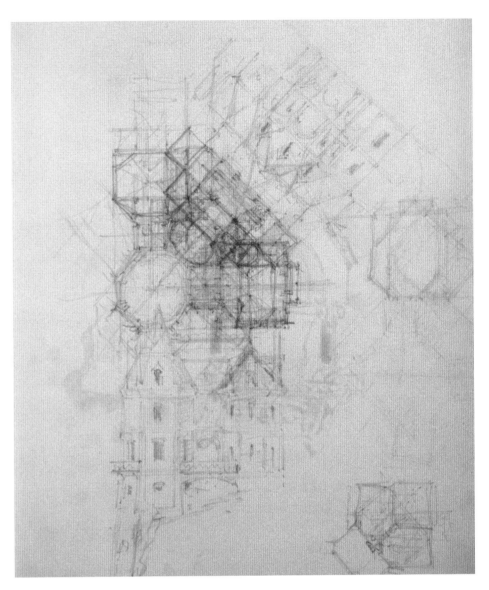

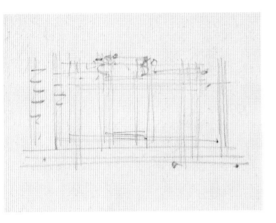

"second-nature"[23] of the Chicago environment, that Wright's great illumination is winnowed out, organically, from this vision of land division rather than inserted into it. The house plans become "figures" in the "ground" of this man-made topography.

There is one immediate difference between Wright's and Sullivan's sketches: In the former the "figure"—that is, the house plan—harmonizes with the ground, the suburban grid, to the point of seeming an emanation of it; while in the latter the figure dominates to the point of the ground disappearing, precisely as Wright was to observe of Sullivan's ornament in 1928, "There was no sense of background, as such, anywhere."[24] Now, if drawing really *was* the architect's work in building-making, if it really was a substitute for organically conceived manual construction like a metaphor acted out, then this distinction is important. I would suggest that it enacts at least three basic distinctions between Wright's and Sullivan's work. First, that Wright repeatedly emphasized drawing his ornament out of materials, while Sullivan imposed ornament on them, always in his personal vocabulary.[25] Second, that Wright's buildings seek to accommodate their landscape situation, while Sullivan's impose themselves, rock-like, in square masses—most impressively at the end of his career in small-town banks. Third, that Wright and Sullivan had different attitudes toward their surrounding society, Wright playing upon it actively throughout his career, Sullivan retreating into Olympian seclusion when work ceased to come and find him after 1900. I would also add a fourth distinction that brings things back to the pure graphicism of drawing: the distinction between Wright's gridding in the construction of his designs and Sullivan's "spinning"—two traditional draftsman's practices, the first (Fig. 7) the quiet and careful rubbing away of segments of a linear matrix laid down initially to leave a solution as a remainder by emphasizing certain lines, the second (Fig. 8) the passionate discovery of a solution in a dense web of counter-designs out of which it is made to emerge.[26]

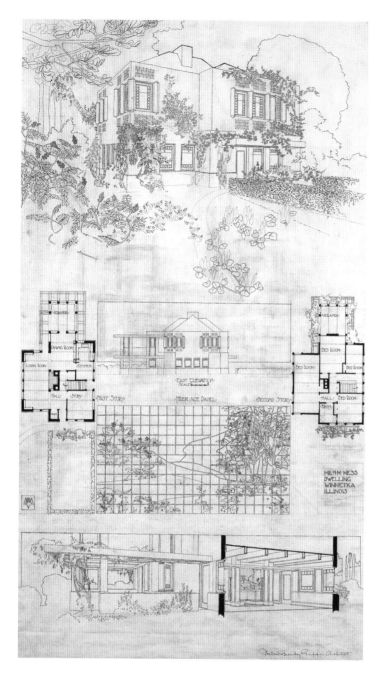

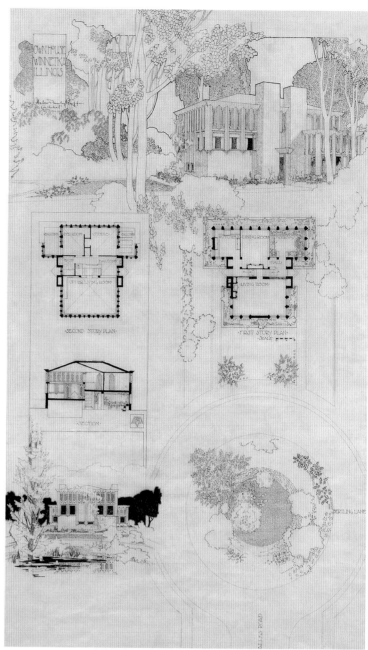

Sullivan's drawing (Fig. 3) only suggests a city plan—it embodies the ultimate "flicker" in scale shifting back and forth between a piece of ornament 24 by 30 inches and the whole world, visible from the Chicago Loop office windows. But in a drawing of 1911–12 by two of Sullivan's firmest admirers (and Wright's former collaborators), Walter Burley Griffin and Marion Mahony Griffin, we see a city plan that won first place in the competition for the plan of Australia's new capital, Canberra.

In the case of the Canberra sheet, however, the architect/renderer (or delineator) is disaggregated between husband (planner) and wife (renderer). It is interesting to see what happened between *her* imagining and *his* execution in the instance of the Mess House of early 1912 (Fig. 9). Here in Marion Mahony Griffin's rendering is a compact prism elaborated into basaltic crystals at the second floor, her silk presentation drawing further elaborated into prismatic decorative fields above and below the windows, this final level of repetition disappearing in the final working drawings.[27] That is, here is a point where these imbricated layers of patterning edge into the ephemeral and may or may not achieve architectural reality. More obvious in its intertwining geometries (but perhaps less successful) is the contemporaneous house the Griffins designed for themselves in the Trier Center development off Winnetka Avenue on the North Shore of Chicago (Fig. 10), where the basaltic subtheme is multiplied into stuttering open planes across the faces of two intersecting prisms, scaling down to window screens and up to pairs of piers enframing the two lateral doors.

Wright's buildings are not composed—they are discovered [empfunden] in three dimensions and generated as organic entities. Thus the houses have no distinct facade or front. They come into being like plants and present ever new aspects….[28]

— Curt Behrendt, *Frankfurter Zeitung,* June 30, 1931

9
Walter Burley Griffin, architect; Marion Mahony, delineator, *H. M. Mess Dwelling, Winnetka, Illinois,* 1912, pen and black ink over graphite on drafting linen. Mary and Leigh Block Museum of Art, Northwestern University, gift of Marion Mahony Griffin, 1985.1.109.

10
Walter Burley Griffin, architect; Marion Mahony, delineator, *Walter Burley Griffin's Own House, Winnetka, Illinois,* 1912 (not built), pen and black ink on drafting linen. Mary and Leigh Block Museum of Art, Northwestern University, gift of Marion Mahony Griffin, 1985.1.108.

Recognizing the mediation of drawing in late 19th- and early 20th-century Chicago design produces a new instrumental history of the origin of modernism. In addition it gives us a very different understanding of Chicago's contribution than the early and formative view presented by Sigfried Giedion in *Space, Time and Architecture* (1941).[29] He evoked a city at the edge of the expansion of European culture able to achieve, undisturbed, organicist virtue of a Ruskinian kind, if under social conditions that he failed to describe. Here instead I am depicting architects finding their managerial and technical way in a city experiencing the same social and philosophical segmentation as elsewhere in the North Atlantic sphere—or in more distant outposts of modernization like Buenos Aires, Tokyo, and Sydney, where, beginning in 1922, the Griffins would build their own "natural" settlement, Castlecrag. This was a culture that fantasized traditional work—Guiraldes or Hudson in Argentina, Thoreau and Whitman in the United States—but functioned through alienated graphic representations.[30]

The peculiar skewing of any craftsmanly well-making we witness in Wright and the Griffins working off Sullivan's volcanic ornamentalism reminds us of the contingentness of Modernism's breakthrough and might inspire a reevaluation of how it all worked. For a moment, just before World War I, Chicago "organic" architecture blended with European experiments and colonial executions: In 1909 Wright visited Europe and in 1910 published his *Ausgeführte Bauten,* and then, starting in 1912, started building in Japan; in 1912 the Griffins won the Canberra competition, toured Europe the next year with their drawings following them the year after at exhibitions in Paris and Lyon (meant to continue to Vienna, but stopped by World War I), before they settled in Australia, then India.[31] European architects came in the other direction, Hendrik Petrus Berlage to visit Chicago in 1911, Rudolph Schindler and Antonin Raymond to work for Wright and stay respectively in 1914 and 1916, followed by Richard Neutra and Werner Moser to work for Wright in 1922 and 1923, and Erich Mendelsohn and Walter Gropius visiting in 1924 and 1926. The critics built an analysis of Chicago modernism, starting with the Dutchmen Berlage (1912), Jan Wils (1916), J. J. P. Oud (1924), and Theodor Wijdeveld (1925/1926)—*De Stijl* published Unity Temple in its second issue (1917)—followed by the more ponderous German constructions of Heinrich De Fries (1926) and Curt Behrendt (1931).[32] The key to understanding Wright for this last author was organic generation, as he makes evident in the quotation heading this section.

Behrendt, as well as his European contemporaries, nonetheless took refuge in a metaphor, the building as a plant—the metaphor Sullivan first focused on in his readings of Spencer around 1881. Giedion (as well as earlier Dutch commentators) modified this into the metaphor of the neatly fitted machine. But what they missed was the mediation of drawing—the issue established by Sullivan and struggled with by Wright and the Griffins was the building drawn like a plant, into a composition of ornamental, efflorescent figures against shimmering grounds. It is this that constitutes the enabling quality of these Chicago designs—their indeterminacy and "flicker" as plan, ornament, and urban map intertwine, and figure and grounds struggle for the dominance, given life by their designers' submergence in the culture of drawing.

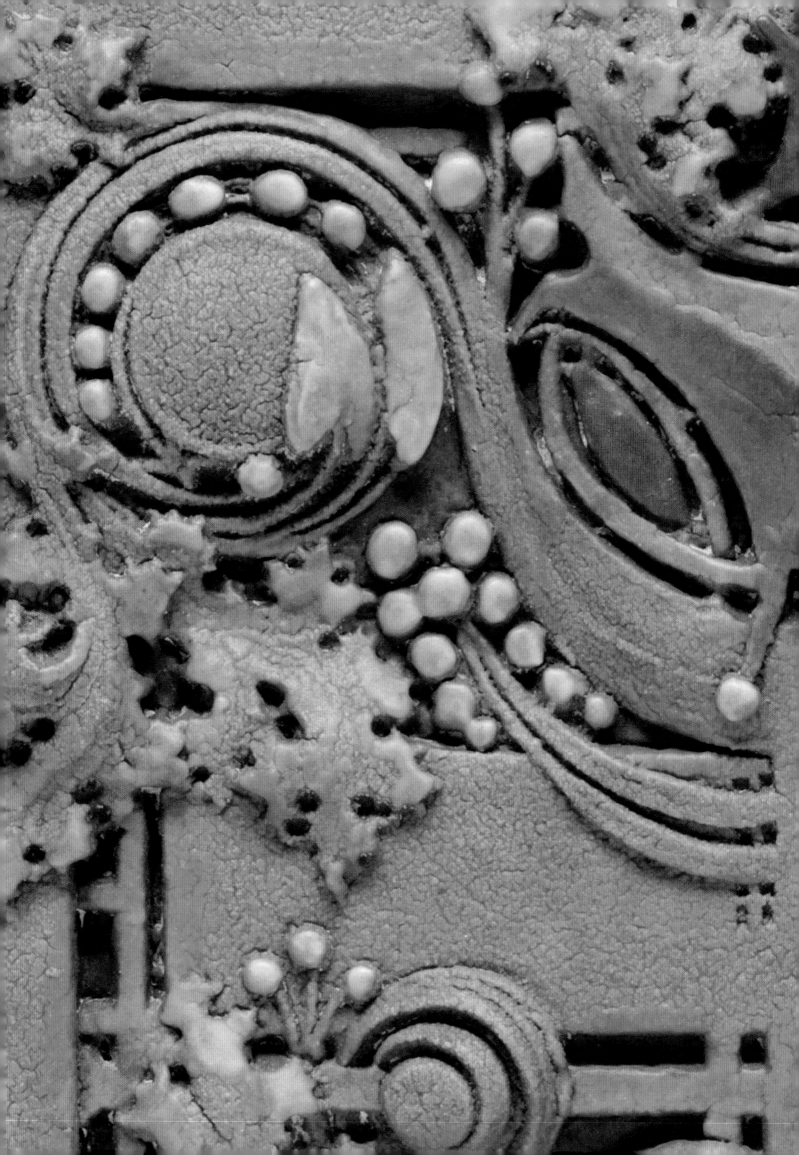

Designing

Evolution: Darwin's

Illustrations

Jacob W. Lewis

Most books Charles Darwin published in his lifetime included illustrations. In *The Origin of Species* (1859) Darwin included a single illustration (see page 3), a schematic model of his theory of evolution that illustrates how related species in a large genus over thousands of generations and multiple mutations evolved into new species, even new genera.[1] While *Origin of Species* contained only one abstract diagram, Darwin's later study *The Expression of the Emotions in Man and Animals* (1872) included 30 heliotypes—a kind of photographic print—along with several wood engravings. He viewed the photographs as support for the book's central thesis, namely, that human behavior was derived from biological processes that human beings shared with their animal ancestors.

From *Origin of Species* onward, the design of Darwin's books had an important role in his scientific work, articulating the theory of natural selection to Victorian readers. The illustrations for Darwin's books represented the concept of contingency—the idea that an organism's survival depended upon external conditions in a perpetual state of change. Darwin's works often addressed the interdependent relationship between different species—between insects and flowers, or earth-worms and mold, for instance—which highlighted the significance of contingency in survival and evolution. As Jonathan Smith has recently written in *Charles Darwin and Victorian Visual Culture*, Darwin faced a "very basic visual problem: how could natural selection, a concept almost by definition impossible to illustrate directly, be illustrated, especially when the existing visual con-ventions of the natural sciences were associated in varying degrees with conceptions of species fixity?"[2] Darwin's insurmountable task was to represent evolution, a glacially slow process, in the *here and now* of the physical book and his own culture. By incorporating pictures and innovative design, Darwin gave his arguments a concrete dimension suitable for large audiences versed in the norms of scientific visual culture.

Darwin was notably eclectic in the kinds of visual evidence he used. Most often, his texts were illustrated with wood engravings, a popular medium that was inexpensive to print. The sources of engraved imagery varied, and many of the botanical illustrations in his books had been published previously. In Darwin's 1862 study of orchids and cross-fertilization, he mined sources such as John Lindley's 1846 study *The Vegetable Kingdom,* reproducing them with little, if any, alteration.[3] In the same book Darwin also modified previously published illustrations in botanical treatises to better fit his focus. In the case of the European common twayblade *(Listera ovata)*, Darwin modified longtime friend and botanist Joseph Dalton Hooker's initial drawing, discussing his changes in a letter to Hooker in September 1860.[4] Darwin's apparent disinterest in composing new images, however, belies the complicated decision-making process that distinguished the design of his books.

Even the simplest of illustrations reveals Darwin's investment in design. The graph in *Origin of Species* presented a purely theoretical claim that moved beyond mere positivism—the belief in verifiable facts and laws based on observation. Representing the survival and extinction of a set of related species over time, the diagram charts the evolution of contemporary species (represented at the top of the diagram) from their mostly extinct ancestors (represented by A through L at the bottom). This sole illustration in *Origin of Species* was not just a diagrammatic supplement to the text; its form resembles a cross section of geological strata, charting where older fossils, perhaps of extinct life forms, had been preserved in the passage of time. Interestingly, the reference to geology calls attention to the lack of evidence to support Darwin's theory, namely, the incomplete fossil record. In effect, Darwin fills the gaps and connects each variation into a regularized and continuous record, representing what he labels the "great Tree of Life."[5]

The image of the tree, with its branches connoting the evolutionary track of animals sharing a common ancestry, continued to fascinate Darwin. Throughout his career he returned again and again to the arboreal metaphor in his efforts to represent evolution. As images to match his words, however, he used illustrations that functioned as symbolic representations rather than what we now consider scientific evidence. These symbolic representations were visual arguments pitched to popular and scientific audiences. Furthermore, Darwin's illustrations were directed especially toward his opponents, the partisans of natural theology, who believed that evidence for the existence of God is found not in revelation but in the natural world.

In Victorian culture science maintained a dialogue with aesthetics, as testified by designers and architects and their views on the life sciences.[6] The designer Christopher Dresser wrote botanical treatises before his involvement with design reform and with what would become the "South Kensington System," a stylistic and pedagogical movement that grew out of the exhibition of arts and manufactures at the Great Exhibition of 1851. His linear and diagrammatically flat renditions of plant forms operate in the vein of what is sometimes called "indirect imitation" of nature— also called the "conventional" approach, a concept discussed at length by Richard Redgrave, inspector general of art in the government-sponsored Art and Science Department, antecedent of the South Kensington Museum.[7] Dresser, like his mentor Redgrave, held the belief that one could arrive at the archetypal forms of plant life and discover their abstract laws of development through the process of observation, comparison, and graphic distillation. Illustrating the principle of "unity in variety," Dresser employed linear abstraction to show the perfect form of plants, which were identified through the comparative study of individual plant specimens.[8] Various contingencies such as weather and sunlight, Dresser argued, interrupted the laws of growth designed by God. Dresser charged botanists with brushing aside what he considered obscuring detritus in order to reveal each specimen's perfect state; designers, he wrote, "are not to draw particular plants as they really exist—blown about and deformed, but as we know them to be" in their pure, untouched state.[9]

The botanical images used by Darwin share affinities with the conventional approach employed by artists in the design reform movement. In his book *The Different Forms of Flowers on Plants of the Same Species* (1877), Darwin emphasized the variety of plant organisms within a species and their dependence on insects for cross-fertilization. Yet most of the accompanying illustrations, like the spare graphic representations showing the two variant flowers such as the cowslip *(Primula veris)* (Fig. 1), read as typological analyses rather than demonstrations of fertilization. The illustrations that do specify process (Fig. 2) leave out any indication of insects, the agents responsible for transferring pollen between variant flowers. Here is where we see the divide between illustration and argumentation in the work of Darwin: The illustrations he provides for his treatise on flower variation omit key elements of the pollination process and method. When placed in a taxonomical study, these illustrations would operate as evidence of separate characteristics of flower varieties.[10] Darwin's illustrations reproduce the conventions of botanical illustration practiced by art botanists, whose beliefs in species fixity and "unity in variety" stood in opposition to the evolutionist's efforts to explain contingency.

If his study on pollination of variant flowers lacked the visual approximation of contingency—in particular the interdependent relations between insects and plant—it was visually addressed in a slightly earlier text, *The Movement and Habits of Climbing Plants* (1875). One illustration resulted from an experiment where Darwin charted the movement of a common pea plant over a small time span by marking its growth on a corresponding plate of glass (Fig. 3). As Jonathan Smith has suggested, the resulting irregular pattern in Darwin's illustration can be read as a reaction to the visual evidence of adherents to the doctrines of natural theology, who by means of deductive reasoning concluded that growth in nature was the product of God-given law—logical,

1
"Primula Veris" (Fig. 1), from Charles Darwin, *The Different Forms of Flowers on Plants of the Same Species* (New York: D. Appleton and Company, 1877). Northwestern University Library.

2
Legitimate Union (Fig. 2), in Charles Darwin, *The Different Forms of Flowers on Plants of the Same Species* (New York: D. Appleton and Company, 1877). Northwestern University Library.

3
"Chart of a Common Pea Plant" (Fig. 6), illustration by George Darwin from Charles Darwin, *The Movement and Habits of Climbing Plants*, second edition (New York: D. Appleton and Company, 1876). Northwestern University Library.

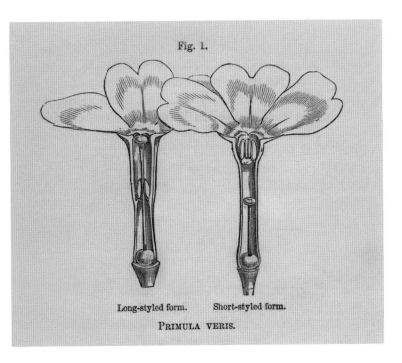

Fig. 1.

Long-styled form.   Short-styled form.

PRIMULA VERIS.

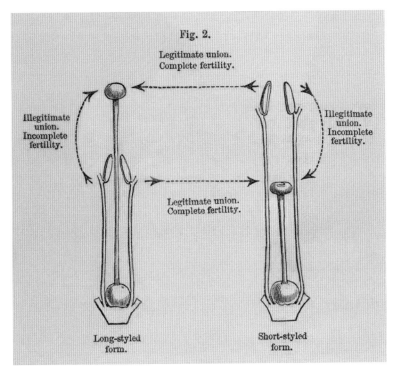

Fig. 2.

Legitimate union.
Complete fertility.

Illegitimate
union.
Incomplete
fertility.

Illegitimate
union.
Incomplete
fertility.

Legitimate union.
Complete fertility.

Long-styled
form.   Short-styled
form.

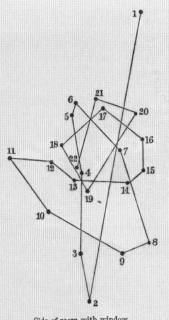

Side of room with window.

Fig. 6.

Diagram showing the movement of the upper internode of the common Pea, traced on a hemispherical glass, and transferred to paper; reduced one-half in size. (Aug. 1st.)

No.				H. M.		No.				H. M.		No.				H. M.	
1	.	.	.	8 46	A.M.	9	.	.	.	1 55	P.M.	16	.	.	.	5 25	P.M.
2	.	.	.	10 0	,,	10	.	.	.	2 25	,,	17	.	.	.	5 50	,,
3	.	.	.	11 0	,,	11	.	.	.	3 0	,,	18	.	.	.	6 25	,,
4	.	.	.	11 37	,,	12	.	.	.	3 30	,,	19	.	.	.	7 0	,,
5	.	.	.	12 7	P.M.	13	.	.	.	3 48	,,	20	.	.	.	7 45	,,
6	.	.	.	12 30	,,	14	.	.	.	4 40	,,	21	.	.	.	8 30	,,
7	.	.	.	1 0	,,	15	.	.	.	5 5	,,	22	.	.	.	9 15	,,
8	.	.	.	1 30	,,												

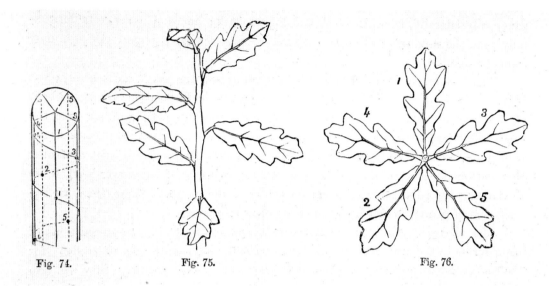

Fig. 74.   Fig. 75.   Fig. 76.

4
"Botanical Growth" (Figs. 74–76),
from Christopher Dresser,
Principles of Decorative Design
(London; New York: Cassell,
Peter, & Galpin, 1873). Charles
Deering McCormick Library of
Special Collections, Northwestern
University Library.

5
"Viola Canina. Fast Sketch, to
show Grouping of Leaves"
(Plate 9), in John Ruskin,
*Proserpina: Studies of Wayside
Flowers* (New York: International
Book Company, n.d.). Charles
Deering McCormick Library of
Special Collections, Northwestern
University Library.

6
"Flora Danica" (Fig. 1), in John
Ruskin, *Proserpina: Studies of
Wayside Flowers* (New York:
International Book Company, n.d.).
Northwestern University Library.

PLATE IX.—VIOLA CANINA.

Fast Sketch, to show Grouping of Leaves.

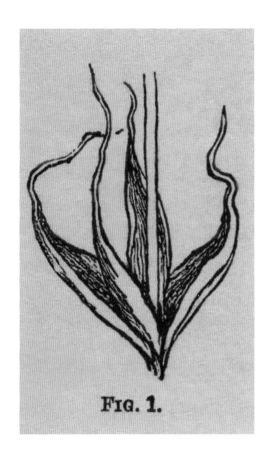

FIG. 1.

mathematical, and common to all plant life.[11] Darwin's illustrations in this volume were in stark contrast to those by Dresser. For example, in his book *The Art of Decorative Design* (1862) and subsequent editions published as *Principles of Decorative Design*, Dresser produced a series of illustrations of botanical growth that charted an individual plant's conformity to a perfect upward spiral (Fig. 4). Although the plant represented in the middle appears irregular and singular, "a principle of order can yet be distinctly traced in the manner of [its] arrangement," Dresser wrote in *Principles of Decorative Design*.[12] In contrast, his chart of the plant's movement communicates the relational dynamic between an individual plant and changes in its external conditions (i.e., sunlight). Through his illustrations Darwin challenged the notion of a plant's internal logic by evidencing its contingent situation. While Dresser sought to represent a plant's perfect state "unmodified by external influences,"[13] Darwin stressed the very influences Dresser disregarded.

Like Darwin, the artist and writer John Ruskin sought to express an individual plant form's singularity within nature, yet the two writers' views on what defined nature stood in direct opposition. One of Darwin's most vocal critics, Ruskin criticized scientists busying themselves with "obscene processes and prurient apparitions" such as the plant's reproductive and digestive processes. These ignoble details of nature, Ruskin railed,

… have furnished the microscopic malice of botanists with providentially disgusting reasons, or demonically nasty necessities, for every possible spur, spike, jag, sting, rent, blotch, flaw, freckle, filth, or venom, which can be detected in the construction, or distilled in the dissolution, of vegetable organism.[14]

For the moralist Ruskin, a full appreciation of nature was grounded in the aesthetic and moral capacity of the viewer, not in the will of the botanist to abstract plants from their natural appearance in the ground and dissect them in the lab. To reduce the variegated splendor of nature to what he considered vulgar processes—the very focus of Darwin's attention—was to degrade nature's divine character and creativity.

An alternative interest in contingency that differs from Darwin's works is manifest in Ruskin's studies of nature. Ruskin's intricate and beautiful renderings of plants and leaves (Fig. 5) read like portraits in their particularity, registering a living form's beauty by calling attention to its fortuitous and irregular details. Observational drawing was a skill Ruskin knew Darwin lacked, indicating to him that Darwin had neither an aesthetic nor moral appreciation of nature.[15] Ruskin offered a contrasting vision of contingency, emphasizing the beautiful over the informational. For him it was the variety of life that conveyed the presence of the metaphysical in nature. Darwin's awe before nature was inspired by the successive adaptation, survival, and reproduction of all living forms over the immense reach of time.[16]

Ruskin's botanical works, collected under the title *Proserpina* in a series of short studies published between 1875 and 1886, constituted an alternative approach to botany geared to a young audience. Unlike the practitioner of botanical morphology, Ruskin observed and sketched live specimens in the open air, resulting in wood engravings for publication. Like Ruskin's watercolors, the wood engravings (carved by Arthur Burgess) in *Proserpina* endow plants with their individual aspects, particularly weathered but resilient leaves (Fig. 6).

In his study of *Climbing Plants*, Darwin demonstrated some affinities with Ruskin's approach in representing aspects of a single organism. Attention to naturalistic form marks a particular wood engraving of the Virginia creeper vine *(Ampelopsis heteracea)* (Fig. 7), made after a drawing by one of his sons. The image, moving in time from one branch to another, illustrates the difference between a young, supple branch and an older spirally contracted one. When some of the young vine's branches fail to grip the wall's surface, Darwin notes in the text, the unused portions wither and drop off, leaving the arms of the older specimen to attach themselves to the wall. His image reads as a morbid contrast in tone to the illustration of a budding primrose *(Primula acaulis*, cousin to the aforementioned cowslip) in Ruskin's *Proserpina* (Fig. 8), which shows the gradual maturation of a flower over time. Whereas Ruskin focused on the more beautiful portion of the plant, Darwin reveled in the constancy of plants struggling for survival. Ruskin's distaste for modern science addressed in *Proserpina* appears to react to larger shifts in scientific knowledge as epito-

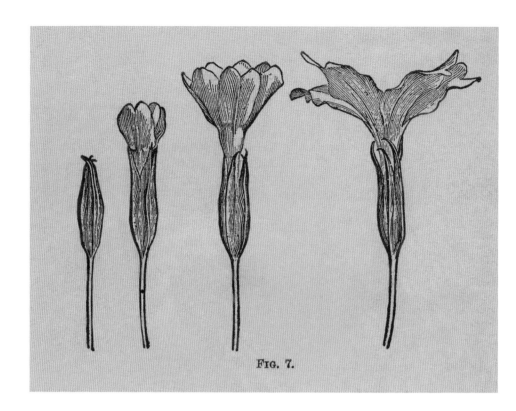

FIG. 7.

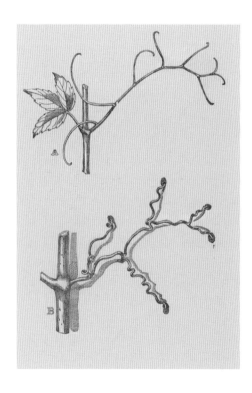

mized by Darwin. The Virginia creeper illustration is evidence of a type of science focusing, Ruskin believed, on the extremes of Victorian society he found increasingly prevalent and socially dangerous: sex, death, disease, and physical struggle. While both Ruskin and Darwin were socially and politically conservative, Darwin's theories hinted at the significance of historical rupture and revolution over the security of tradition and religion.

Darwin's vines may be considered a microcosmic test case for his theory at large, a metaphorical image of natural selection. The text shows his appreciation for those same vines climbing the exterior of his house: "The gain in strength and durability in a tendril after its attachment is something wonderful. There are tendrils now adhering to my house which are still strong, and have been exposed to the weather in a dead state for 14 or 15 years."[17] The image and his description implicitly recall the "Tree of Life" (see page 3), Darwin's illustration from *Origin of Species* that was rooted in biblical metaphor and, in the 19th century, employed by proponents of natural theology. Although the approaches of natural theology and evolution remained radically dissimilar, Darwin made his case in *Origin of Species* for the appropriateness of the metaphor:

I believe this simile [of the tree] largely speaks the truth. The green and budding twigs may represent existing species; and those produced during each former year may represent the long succession of extinct species. At each period of growth all the growing twigs have tried to branch out on all sides, and to overtop and kill the surrounding twigs and branches, in the same manner as species and groups of species have tried to overmaster other species in the great battle for life.... As buds give rise by growth to fresh buds, and these, if vigorous, branch out and overtop on all sides many a feebler branch, so by generation I believe it has been with the great Tree of Life, which fills with its dead and broken branches the crust of the earth, and covers the surface with its ever branching and beautiful ramifications.[18]

This text and the later one from *Climbing Plants* demonstrated Darwin's lasting preoccupation with not only the branches that survive but also those that are cast off. The language of metaphor and wonder that pervades his initial text on evolution held significance throughout his career. The contest he saw between the stronger branches and the ones that failed to survive spoke to the larger significance of contingency in the process of evolution.

Just as in his botanical studies, Darwin endeavored to portray animal life and human beings as dependent on the conditions of their environment. His efforts to find a visual equivalent to the phenomena of contingency led him to the use of photography for *The Expression of the Emotions in Man and Animals* (1872). Radical in its conclusions, the book set out to prove that human expression was the result of animal ancestry, the evidence of which was observable by comparing animal and human behavior and physiology.[19] In explaining the persistence of emotional expression due to heredity by natural and sexual selection, Darwin aimed to shift the terms of the debate from a discussion of intelligence, volition, and intention to an interest in the physiological manifestations of emotion acted out by the face and body. His study counters the centuries-old science of physiognomy, which sought to explain an individual's moral character based on external facial expression and bodily pose. Darwin's arguments were also with aesthetics and art, to which physiognomy was closely aligned, and appear in his challenge to the work of Sir Charles Bell and his treatise on human expression in art, *The Anatomy and Philosophy of Expression as Connected with the Fine Arts*, first published in 1806 and then rewritten for an 1844 edition.[20]

Originally planning the treatise as a chapter in *The Descent of Man* (1871), Darwin opted to give the subject of human expression its own lengthy treatment. In search of evidence to support his claims, he first turned to the fine arts but found little evidence he could use, given that beauty remained art's "chief object."[21] Just as his inadequate draftsmanship made him a critical target for Ruskin, Darwin's summary dismissal of aesthetics and art history only fueled critics. In a lengthy review published in the Whig-sympathetic *Edinburgh Review*, T. S. Baynes attacked (among other things) the type of inductive scientific reasoning practiced by Darwin and other modern scientists. Yet the most pointed invective offered by Baynes had to do with the book's dearth of consideration for art: "Mr. Darwin apparently knows nothing of art," he wrote, "and certainly has no perception of its intimate relation to the subject he undertakes to expound."[22] Further along in the review, the critic offered Darwin a short lesson in art history: "Expression is the very point by which modern art is so broadly and decisively separated from ancient art," which was believed, since Johann Winckelmann, to represent and manifest aspects of the beautiful.[23] According to Baynes, the chief objective of modern art—here meaning art since the Renaissance—was not beauty but expression. Baynes thought that Darwin unduly dismissed an entire category of evidence by defining art in terms of beauty alone.

In countering prevailing aesthetic understanding Darwin searched for new ways to represent the mechanics of expression. As he relates in his introduction: "The study of expression is difficult, owing to the movements being often extremely slight, and of a fleeting nature... When we witness any deep emotion, our sympathy is so strongly excited that close observation is forgotten or rendered almost impossible."[24] Thinking photography to be the perfect *aide memoire* in the study of human expression, he spent three years gathering photographs from commercial vendors in the same way he collected natural specimens.[25] George Wallich, known for his somewhat slick portraits of children, was the first photographer Darwin commissioned to capture states of emotion in children, but the results proved unsatisfactory, and only one photograph by Wallich made it into the book.

Sometime in 1871 Darwin met photographer Oscar Rejlander, perhaps through their mutual friend, art photographer Julia Margaret Cameron.[26] Although Rejlander was initially deferential to the divide separating the fine arts from the technology of photography, he later argued that photography was an art in its own right, making him an odd candidate to illustrate Darwin's study.[27] Darwin was impressed in particular with Rejlander's studies of children and commissioned him to photograph them crying. With the photographs Darwin attempted to link the instinctual emotions of children with the more habitual emotions expressed by adults. It was Darwin's hope that Rejlander would capture—"by the instantaneous process" of photography—a precise moment of agitation, when the child's mouth opened wide and the flesh around the eyes became flush with blood.[28] Despite the limitations of the technology (exposures required several seconds), Darwin counted as one among many who thought the photograph was capable of fixing fleeting actions before technological improvements led to what could accurately be named instantaneous photography. For Darwin photography had the potential to demonstrate a moment in time, what Walter Benjamin has called "the tiny spark of contingency, of the here and now" that connects a viewer with a certain past moment, preserved in a photograph.[29]

The book's first heliotype is probably Rejlander's most effective (Fig. 9), but neither Darwin nor Rejlander admitted to its complicated production history.[30] Rejlander's initial photograph of the child lacked the detail necessary for reproduction as a heliotype.[31] The artist then made an

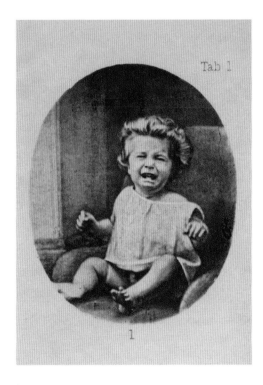

9
O. G. Rejlander, Fig. 1
(Plate 1), from Charles Darwin,
The Expression of the Emotions in Man and Animals
(New York and London:
D. Appleton and Company,
1872). Northwestern University Library.

10
O. G. Rejlander, Fig. 1 (Plate 7), from Charles Darwin, *The Expression of the Emotions in Man and Animals* (New York and London: D. Appleton and Company, 1873). Northwestern University Library.

11
O. G. Rejlander, Fig. 1 (Plate 4), in Charles Darwin, *The Expression of the Emotions in Man and Animals* (New York and London: D. Appleton and Company, 1873). Northwestern University Library.

enlargement in chalk and subsequently rephotographed the drawing, emphasizing certain facial muscles and concealing other areas of the body with shading, notably the child's genitals. He even altered the setting: Instead of the original photograph's flat platform, Rejlander included a cozy chair in an effort to authenticate the experiment by staging it in a domestic environment, as if the child cried spontaneously at home. The new signs of contingency that Darwin wanted—individual presence and spontaneity—were not actually captured but meticulously constructed through deliberate exclusions and alterations.

No doubt due in part to the apparent spontaneity conveyed by the staged photograph, the image of the crying child became popular and was dubbed "Ginx's Baby," after Edward Jenkins's popular novel of the same name.[32] Jenkins's story followed the life of a child born to a poor London family who after successive misfortunes drowns himself in the Thames. Despite its initial scientific use, Rejlander's photograph provoked public sympathy and encouraged alternative readings from bourgeois moralists and social activists alike.[33] Darwin's illustrations were the object of what might be considered competing contingencies: Political debates about Britain's poor, for instance, crept into interpretations of Rejlander's fake photograph.

In an effort to match Darwin's wish for unmediated access to spontaneous movements and expressions, Rejlander's photographs of adults in certain states of emotion adopt the conventions of theater. Rejlander (Fig. 10) and his wife (Fig. 11), among others, simulated expressions by theatrical poses before a camera, which worked against Darwin's initial faith in photography as an objective medium. While in the text he is careful to note that the photographs only approximate real emotions, Darwin manages to conflate illustration with evidence in the photographs, as noted by one book reviewer in *The Athenaeum*:

These photographs are sufficient to illustrate Mr. Darwin's meaning; but they have no higher value. The more we look at them, the less satisfactory do they appear. We are far from thinking that Mr. Darwin has acted unwisely in introducing them into his book, but Mr. Rejlander's performances are almost sure to mislead any one who puts much faith in them.[34]

In his challenge to the dominion of aesthetics, Darwin's photographic illustrations in the end staged science rather than introduced to the discipline a new form of evidence. In spite of the allure of its apparent mechanical objectivity, the photograph was not synonymous with authenticity, and some critics remained skeptical of photography's truth-telling capabilities.[35]

FIG. 5.—Dog approaching another dog with hostile intentions. By Mr. Riviere.

While Rejlander's contribution garnered the most remarks by reviewers, the book con-
tains various contributors and types of illustration, ranging from wood engravings of animals by
Thomas Wood (Fig. 12) to photographs of Dr. G. B. Duchenne de Boulogne's experiments in facial
muscle stimulation, most notably on an older man with facial paralysis (Fig. 13). In some instances
photographs were copied as wood engravings, such as Duchenne's photograph illustrating the
expression of terror (Fig. 14). In the 1850s, as a clinician at the Salpêtrière asylum outside Paris,
Duchenne performed experiments on participants using a galvanizing tool to shoot current into a
subject's face to sustain expressions for the long exposure times necessitated by the camera. In
translating the photograph, the engraver for Darwin's book omitted the galvanizing tool visible
in the photograph, making the expression and his muscular contractions more legible and prominent.[36] The artist's manipulation of the image, however, becomes apparent when viewed with the
rest of Duchenne's images in Darwin's study: The galvanizing tool appears in all but this illustration. As Carol Armstrong has suggested, the omission was due to Darwin's unease with having
viewers think that the expression of terror was only the result of the proximity of the galvanizing
tool, despite the experimental (albeit exploitative) environment controlled by Duchenne.[37]

It is easy to criticize the deliberate staging of science in Rejlander's theatrical simula-
tions, Duchenne's artificial experiments, and Darwin's conflation of evidence with illustration in
Expression of the Emotions. Photography constituted only one strategy, however, in Darwin's
efforts to represent contingency. His illustrations for *Climbing Plants* and the earlier "Tree of Life"
diagram are symbolic representations when viewed in the context of his writing, just as Rejlander's
performances exploited the public's suppositions about the spontaneity of photography in order
to represent human expression frozen at an instant. Darwin's representational strategies came at a
time when neither language nor visual technology afforded him a systematic means of expressing
his theories. Working together, however, word and image approximated the idea of contingency
that was so important to his theory of evolution.

A culminant moment in his efforts to represent contingency perhaps can be found in
his illustrations for his last book, *The Formation of Vegetable Mould through the Action of Worms*
(1881). Like his study of variant flowers, his study of mold adds to his explanation of the dependence between species in an environment. Two illustrations show the mold that gathers around
worm "castings" or droppings (Fig. 15). Such strange forms, and Darwin's preoccupation with them,

14

"Terror" (Fig. 20), engraving
after a photograph by G. B.
Duchenne, in Charles Darwin,
*The Expression of the Emo-
tions in Man and Animals*
(New York and London:
D. Appleton and Company,
1873). Northwestern University Library.

15

"A tower-like casting, probably ejected by a species of
Perichaeta, from the Botanic
garden, Calcutta; of natural
size" (Fig. 3), engraving after
a photograph, in Charles
Darwin, *The Formation of
Vegetable Mould, through
the Action of Worms, with
Observations on Their Habits*
(New York: D. Appleton & Co.,
1911). Northwestern University Library.

FIG. 20.—Terror, from a photograph by Dr. Duchenne.

demonstrate the extreme of what Ruskin called the "obscene processes and prurient apparitions" that interested modern scientists.[38] The illustrations were engraved after photographs, and the translation gives them an otherworldly character. Not only are they instances of real things that had been photographed, they also stand isolated in engravings as if objects of monumental impor- tance. Here the engraver utilized a kind of photographic, authenticating realism in his rendering of a repulsive yet fascinating object.[39]

For Darwin, the worm castings also served as objects of reflection on the temporality of nature and the cyclical state of the world, as he writes in the book's conclusion:

When we behold a wide, turf-covered expanse, we should remember that its smoothness, on which so much of its beauty depends, is mainly due to all the inequalities having been slowly leveled by worms. It is a marvelous reflection that the whole of the superficial mould over any such expanse has passed, and will again pass, every few years through the bodies of worms.[40]

Just as in *Expression of the Emotions*, Darwin returns to the question of aesthetics in his study of worms and mold, here stating that the beauty of a pastoral landscape—"a wide, turf-covered expanse"—is contingent on the digestive processes of worms. Not only is beauty contingent on the worms; human history itself is made to look inconsequential when compared with the importance of the earthworm:

The plough is one of the most ancient and most valuable of man's inventions; but long before he existed the land was in fact regularly ploughed, and still continues to be thus ploughed by earth- worms. It may be doubted whether there are many other animals which have played so important a part in the history of the world, as have these lowly organized creatures.[41]

With respect to the conclusion, the book's few illustrations of worm castings appear as if they were monuments built by an ancient civilization, as Jonathan Smith has written.[42] Yet the relevance of these two prints to evolutionary theory can also be seen in the design process by which Darwin communicates the concept of contingency in various ways. Alongside the book's focus, detailing the correlation between worm digestion and mold, as well as his more poetic ruminations on the connections between earthworms and civilization, the photographic presentation of the castings communicate to the viewer that these objects exist and take on readable, distinguishable features. Darwin even used the photographs to compare his own specimens with those documented in Calcutta.[43]

Like the "Tree of Life" and the image of the Virginia creeper, with the illustrations of lowly worm droppings Darwin once again found a symbolic representation of his theories, which hinged on processes of contingency and struggle, no matter how perverse the subject. Darwin used visual representation as a means of argumentation, if not always successfully in the eyes of his critics, who ranged from the eloquent yet vociferous Ruskin to those who challenged the very mode of illustration used in *Expression of the Emotions*. Nevertheless, Darwin's verbal acuity necessitated a visual corollary, and his involvement in book design and illustration attests to his own struggle in the world of 19th-century science and the popular imagination. Needless to say, he adapted well to both.

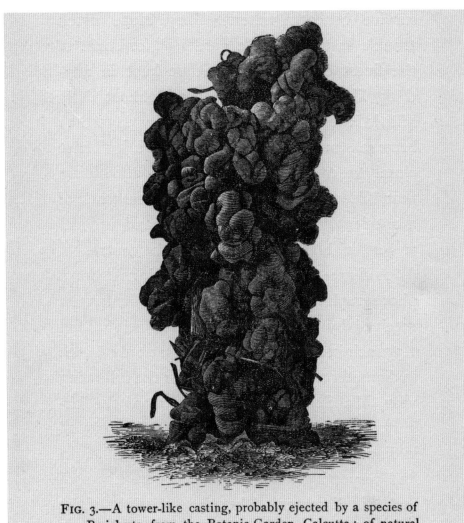

FIG. 3.—A tower-like casting, probably ejected by a species of Perichæta, from the Botanic Garden, Calcutta ; of natural size, engraved from a photograph.

Evolution and Homogenic Love in C. R. Ashbee's Guild of Handicraft

Angelina Lucento

C. R. [Charles Robert] Ashbee was not a man of science. Trained first as a historian and then as an architect, Ashbee remained throughout his life deeply committed to the humanistic disciplines of art and philosophy and strove to formulate a practical philosophy of aesthetics that would foster the development of a socialist society free of the poverty and materialism brought on by industrial capitalism. Nevertheless, both Ashbee's writings and his designs reflect and express a belief that, in order to attain the socialist ideal, the human race must adapt to its constantly changing environment and that those adaptations be passed on to future generations. Ashbee's general understanding of social evolution is therefore closer to that of French biologist Jean-Baptiste Lamarck than Charles Darwin. Indeed, he incorporated elements of the former's theory of adaptation into his own "homogenic" communism, a philosophy he used to thwart the widespread Social Darwinism of his day and which he put into practice with the Guild of Handicraft.[1]

C. R. Ashbee: Scholarly Beginnings

C. R. Ashbee discovered both radical sex and radical politics at King's College, Cambridge. Reluctant to follow in the footsteps of his father, a successful London merchant, Ashbee went to the university to escape an obligatory apprenticeship in the family business and arrived at King's in 1882 without any particular goals or ambitions. Soon, however, he fell in with a group of young intellectuals that included Goldsworthy Lowes Dickinson, who went on to become a noted historian and pacifist, and the scientist-turned-artist and critic Roger Fry.[2] Together the friends read philosophy and history and often argued about the ideas they found most inspiring. It was through these intense reading and discussion sessions that Ashbee first discovered the works of John Ruskin and William Morris. He began ruminating on humanity's relationship to the natural world and the causes of social ills; Ashbee was especially interested in the communism that he found in Morris's writing.[3] While the ideas proposed by Ruskin and Morris greatly influenced the development of his socialist and artistic philosophies, Ashbee was also introduced, during his years at Cambridge, to a scholar whose work would have an even greater impact on his thought and development: Edward Carpenter. Ashbee not only voraciously consumed the work of Carpenter but met him and established an enduring friendship. Indeed, this lasting relationship was the most significant of Ashbee's career.

In the 1880s Carpenter was a well-known philosopher, historian, and scholar of sexuality. He was also a self-professed Lamarckian.[4] Writing in the early 19th century, Lamarck concluded that the physical characteristics of human beings and other higher animals were modified as the direct result of changes within their external environment.[5] Lamarck argued that when organisms sensed changes in their environment, they developed needs (*besoin*), which he characterized as an "inner feeling" or "wish," that signaled them to physically change in order to successfully adapt to their new environment.[6] Under these circumstances, the organs that proved most useful in the new environment became better developed, while those that were less so began to shrink and atrophy. Lamarck believed not only that these physical changes would quickly manifest themselves within the individual but that they would also be passed along to the individual's offspring.[7] Such modifications, he argued, brought the organism closer to perfection. In his essay "Exfoliation: Lamarck versus Darwin," Carpenter argued against Darwin's theory of natural selection in favor of Lamarck's, calling the Frenchman a "true poet."[8] Carpenter wrote that Darwin's theory was flawed because it failed to account for human agency, the ability of man to develop conscious needs and desires and act upon them.[9] He extrapolated from Lamarck's theory of biological adaptation and evolution to develop an analogous theory of biological and social transformation, which he termed "exfoliation,"

On the theory of Exfoliation, which is practically Lamarck's theory, there is a force at work throughout creation, ever urging each type onward into new and newer forms. This force appears first in the consciousness in the form of *desire*…. As each new desire or ideal is evolved, it brings the creature into conflict with its surroundings, then, gaining its satisfaction, externalizes itself in the structure of the creature, and leaves the way open for the birth of a new ideal.[10]

Love, Carpenter believed, is always at the core of man's desire.[11] Man was motivated above and beyond all else—including the desire for food and rest—by his love for the human form.[12] Desire, therefore, is a dynamic force that drives man to seek physical and mental perfection, to become free of the physical and mental flaws that led to hatred, greed, and struggle against his fellow men. Out of this love for human perfection, man seeks to become a "Super-man."[13] When he finally reaches perfection, so too will society; utopia will finally be achieved.[14]

For the process of exfoliation to culminate in this divine state of existence, Carpenter argued that man must live in close contact with the soil that nourishes his body. He must also live and work in a community with his fellow men, sharing in their friendship and love, for such conditions nurture man's desire, his love of the human body and mind. Only under these circumstances will man's physical and mental characteristics become more perfect; only under these circumstances will he be able to pass those perfected characteristics on to his young.[15] Industrial capitalism, according to Carpenter, with its division of labor and emphasis on supply and demand, forces men away from the land and into the factory; it also erodes the bonds between them by emphasizing individual rather than communal work.[16] Carpenter does not, however, advocate adapting to the conditions of capitalism. On the contrary, since capitalism is an impediment to the fulfillment of human desire, men must return to the land and the commune where physical and mental strength will be increased and passed on to succeeding generations, at which point communism becomes inevitable.[17]

What is interesting about Carpenter's neo-Lamarckian theory of evolution is that it is dependent upon his own unique philosophy of human sexuality. For Ashbee, who had sexual relationships with other men throughout his life, this aspect of Carpenter's work was especially appealing. Carpenter, who was also gay, wrote prolifically about the origin and purpose of what he called "homogenic love."[18] According to Carpenter, homogenic love—or comradeship, as he also sometimes referred to it—was defined as any caring, passionate relationship between two members of the same sex.[19] While Carpenter admitted that such relationships could indeed involve sexual intimacy, he was emphatic in his belief that homogenic love was not limited to sexual relations. In his words, "It would also be a great error to overlook the fact that in a large number of instances the relation is not distinctively sexual at all, though it may be said to be physical in the sense of embrace and endearment."[20] Carpenter's contribution to the field of Victorian sexuality studies, however, extended far beyond this particular definition. Citing examples from history, literature, and philosophy, as well as the works of several 19th-century scientists, he also proposed that the tendency toward homogenic love was innate in everyone; women as well as men harbored the potential for the formation of homogenic bonds.[21] More radically, Carpenter proclaimed that the evolution of the Super-man and the development of a socialist society depended wholly upon homogenic love and that its neglect and repression threatened the commonweal:[22]

And beyond the extirpation of evils we have solid work waiting to be done in the patient and life-long building up of new forms of society, new orders of thought, and new institutions of human solidarity…. Such campaigns as these…will call for equahardihood [*sic*] and courage and will stand in need of comradeship as true and valiant.[23]

While he recognized that male-female sexual relations were of course necessary for the survival of the species, Carpenter suggested that the valorization of this relationship, through the social institution of marriage, as the only legitimate type of "love-union" was at least partially responsible for modern society's tendency toward cutthroat capitalism and the social problems associated with it. According to Carpenter,

It is not unlikely that the markedly materialistic and commercial character of the last age of European civilised life is largely to be connected with the fact that the *only* form of love and love-union that is recognised has been one founded on the quite necessary but comparatively materialistic basis of matrimonial sex-intercourse and child-breeding.[24]

Carpenter further explains that by sanctioning a woman becoming the property of her husband through the legal and religious bonds of marriage, capitalist civilization legitimizes the social inequalities it produces.[25] Since homogenic love, on the other hand, involves comradeship between members of the same sex, such relationships never fall prey to male-female gender roles, in which the wife is expected to become subordinate to the husband. In Carpenter's view, homogenic love is an equalizing force capable of eroding the social distinctions that capitalism's sanctioning of heterosexual love and marriage works to shore up.[26]

In addition to recording his philosophical viewpoint in several volumes of written work, Carpenter put his Lamarckian belief in heritable perfectibility into practice by establishing a male commune at Millthorpe, his farm near Sheffield, Yorkshire, where the young Ashbee was a frequent visitor. Impressed by this living example of a small-scale, homogenic society in which men seemed to live close to nature, Ashbee—an intensely practical man who believed that philosophy should lead to concrete endeavors—began to formulate his own scheme for social change. It was based in part upon the works of Ruskin and Morris, but equally upon Carpenter's Lamarckian philosophy of adaptation and homogenic love. Ashbee wrote, suggestively, in his journal upon his return home from a visit to Millthorpe, "Edward's idea [about the need for homogenic love] is still burning within me. I feel so proud that he should have chosen me as a vessel in which to place it."[27] After leaving King's College with a degree in history in 1886, he set off with great enthusiasm on his quest to fulfill that trust.

Further Ideas That Inspired the Guild of Handicraft

After Cambridge, Ashbee moved to the slums of East London. He took up residence in Toynbee Hall, a university settlement that had been established by a group of idealistic Oxford graduates in 1884. The aim of the university settlement movement was to place educated young men in the most impoverished pockets of English society. The hope was their presence among the working class would disrupt the alienating geographical divide between the rich and the poor that characterized London. The university men also sought to raise the educational standards of the masses in the East End by giving free public lectures on art, history, literature, and economics.[28] In the evenings Ashbee lectured on one of his favorite topics, the writings of John Ruskin, and soon became quite popular. During the day he worked as an apprentice architect at the firm of Bodley and Garner. Although he enjoyed his work as both a teacher and an architect, Ashbee was neither satisfied with his life nor Toynbee Hall. Like Ruskin and Morris, Ashbee believed that art not only reflected the inner workings of a particular society but also could be used to change that society. He began to formulate a plan for a kind of art making that he was convinced would be so in harmony with man's innate drive to perfection for himself and for society that it would inevitably lead the worker to a life of happiness, love, and satisfaction.

Living and teaching among the working classes had directly exposed Ashbee to the social ills of urban life in late Victorian England—including poverty, disease, and overcrowding. He became convinced that mechanization and the industrial division of labor were the root causes of all social inequality.[29] Like Ruskin and Morris, Ashbee idealized medieval art and society and was particularly fascinated with that period's workman's guilds, believing them to be exemplary communal systems that did not exploit workers. It was his opinion that the drive to form such guilds, in which the primary purpose of the labor effort was human comradeship and the production of useful objects, was innate in people. Ashbee's study of history, as well as Morris's novel *A Dream of John Ball* (serialized in 1886–87), had a serious impact on the development of this viewpoint. Morris's book is particularly explicit in its description of an innate drive to communal work and mutual cooperation.[30] Additionally, the 19th century's most eloquent spokesman for anarchic communism, the Russian aristocrat Pyotr Kropotkin, immigrated to England in 1886 and began publishing English translations of his works that year; his first article in the widely read journal *Nineteenth Century* was printed in February 1887.[31] Although there is no direct evidence that Ashbee read these essays, knowledge of the Russian emigré's work would have been impossible for him to avoid. Not only was his writing widely discussed and debated in the socialist circles of the 1880s, but Kropotkin had also established a relationship with Edward Carpenter, who, in fact, helped him refine and elaborate his anarchist belief that human beings are naturally inclined toward mutual cooperation and have no need for a central government.[32] Ashbee's interpretation of the impulse to communism, however, had a unique twist: Like Carpenter, he believed that it was always dependent upon and inseparable from man's inclination toward homogenic love.

Ashbee was convinced that manifestations of this inclination could be seen throughout history, and the medieval guilds were his favorite example:

Every average English workman is an idealist.... [T]his side of him finds expression in theoretical socialism. He cons these formulae [of theoretical socialism] over daily in his half-penny paper, much as a medieval workman said his Aves and Paternosters, but they remain to him unreal, phantasmal, insubstantial.... It requires but the igniting spark—the pinch of hunger, for instance, resulting from an unsuccessful war—and all this idealism, so productive if rightly applied towards a national purpose, may blow the whole social faction to pieces.[33]

The idealism that Ashbee refers to here is the impulse toward homogenic, anarchic communism. In his writing he uses neither "idealism" nor "socialism" exclusively but switches between the terms when discussing his philosophies of human nature and social change. The two words function as synonyms; both describe what Ashbee believed to be man's innate impulse to work together with other men, to engage in mutual aid through communal labor. It is notable but not surprising that Ashbee neglected to tack the distinction "homogenic" onto either of these phrases. Carpenter's most radical writings, including his thesis on homogenic love, were published privately as pamphlets and enjoyed only a limited distribution for fear that the general public would interpret them as obscene and that he might be prosecuted. Even when he did not directly invoke the word, Ashbee indicates that homogenic love—in the form of comradeship—is necessary for the successful evolution of an anarchic-socialist society. Indeed, he only ever refers to "socialist" or "idealist" movements that take place among men and repeatedly emphasizes the importance of male comradeship and craft that "brings men together and helps them to live in fellowship."[34] (Women were excluded from these analyses, just as they were later actively excluded from joining the Guild of Handicraft.)

Ashbee was also influenced by the philosopher Herbert Spencer, who coined the phrase "survival of the fittest" and was the father of Social Darwinism. In Spencer's view, the scientific and technological progress that the Industrial Revolution had brought reflected society's advancement toward perfection. Those members of the species, he argued, who were best equipped physically and mentally for the rigors of life in an industrial society would not only survive, they would prosper. Those who were not so well equipped would ultimately succumb to poverty, disease, and vice and thus be eliminated.[35] Spencer was vehemently opposed to governmental aid to the poor, believing that such aid would interfere with what he considered to be society's most effective form of natural selection and obstruct society's march toward perfection.

Ashbee concurred with Spencer's belief that man possesses an innate drive toward progress and perfection, but did not agree with Spencer's theory that this evolution would eventually come about through struggle, capitalist competition, and natural selection. Ashbee believed working-class men were impoverished not as the result of an inherent defect or inability to adapt to capitalism but rather because they failed to recognize and adapt to their innate need for anarchic socialism and homogenic love. Only by living and working in ways that satisfied these needs—

living communally and producing art—would men be able to acquire the characteristics that would allow the wider society to progress toward perfection.

The Birth of the Guild of Handicraft

Drawing on what he had learned from Morris, Ruskin, Kropotkin, and Carpenter, Ashbee formulated his own plan for the transformation of society. In the winter of 1887 he spoke with Carpenter and Morris about the possibility of creating a guild of handicraft in which young men from the East End would engage in the communal production of useful objects. Morris's response was most discouraging. Disillusioned in the wake of political turmoil, he told Ashbee that such a small effort would never be of any use.[36] Carpenter, however, supported the idea and encouraged Ashbee to go forth with his plan. The Guild of Handicraft was formed in the heart of East London in 1888.

From the beginning the Guild had no central governing body; every worker had a share in its profits and a say in decision-making processes.[37] The Guild's design philosophies were in keeping with the tradition of the English Arts and Crafts movement, which began under the influence of William Morris in the early 1870s. The Arts and Crafts movement proposed that since nature was the source for all pattern and raw materials, the craftsman should not produce objects based on designs that obscured or detracted from their inherent properties, such as the grain of wood or the sheen of silver.[38] As the Guildsmen began to produce and sell objects, Ashbee began to believe that he had achieved his goal of revolutionizing the modern English work process—at least on a small scale. By working communally in a workshop setting and sharing the profits, his men were satisfying their natural tendency toward anarchic communism and homogenic love. In language indebted to Carpenter, Ashbee wrote during the Guild's early days that he was "keeping the sacred lamp of the New Socialism always before me…making the bulwarks of real human love so strong in the hearts of our men and boys that no castrated affection shall dare face it."[39] The Guild did not strive for profit; rather its goal was to provide the worker with a comfortable enough existence that he would never have any need or desire to leave and that the community could remain a self-sustaining and self-perpetuating enterprise based upon the principle of homogenic love.

The Guild eventually became quite successful. The objects the men produced sold well, and the system was able to sustain itself very effectively. Ashbee, however, eventually became dissatisfied with the Guild's location. While he understood the importance of being in East London and making the Guild accessible to the population that needed it most, he was disturbed by the fact that the neighborhood had become a place of spectacular entertainment for the bourgeoisie. It was not uncommon to see members of the upper classes traipsing around the streets in groups in order to see the horror of the slums and gape at the degradation of the poor.[40] Ashbee worried that this would be detrimental to both the Guild and his men; he also wanted to bring his men closer to nature. In 1890 he decided to move the operation to Mile End Road on the outer suburbs of the East.[41] The Guild remained at this location, called Essex House, until 1902, and it was here that the operation entered its most productive phase. Many of the objects now extant were made during this period and directly reflect the goals of the Guild.

The Guild's products were, in Ashbee's opinion, of great value to the community. As head designer, Ashbee inspected everything his men produced and made sure that the objects honored the Arts and Crafts tradition by staying true to both the patterns of nature and to the materials from which they had been created. It was important to Ashbee, however, that the objects should somehow reflect the unique personal qualities of the individuals who produced them. While such a stance may seem contradictory to his communist ideas, in fact it was not. A work setting that encouraged men to form a community where they could learn from one another, share certain tasks, and foster their homogenic love was, according to Ashbee, the only type of work environment in which the individual craftsman's creativity could truly blossom:

The life of the producer is to the community a more vital consideration than the cheap production that ignores it, and thus the human and ethical considerations that insist on the individuality of the workman are of the most importance.[42]

Ashbee's Guild was designed to improve the life of the producer by establishing "human and ethical considerations," i.e., anarchic communism and homogenic love. Under these conditions, which "insist on the individuality of the workman," each producer would inevitably create products that reflected his unique character. Ashbee believed that this individuality would be immediately visible to consumers. Whereas the process of rote mechanization that was so common in the industrial context erased every trace of the worker's hand from the final product, the Guildsman's products would always reflect his own hand and his own soul. Although Ashbee eschewed in his workshops an elaborate division of labor, he did not completely reject mechanization itself. While he may have vehemently disagreed with the notion that men could successfully adapt to the living conditions of capitalism, he did believe that the worker and the machine could adapt to one another. In his view, mechanization was simply a sign of dynamism and progress. In keeping with Lamarck's view that man had to adapt to his changing environment in order to survive, Ashbee ensured that his Guildsmen adapted to using machines. As long as men remained master of the machine and did not become subordinate to it, the relationship could actually help destroy the capitalist system.[43] He wrote that when an "idealist" or "socialist" work system was successfully combined with the machine, "planning and building up of the new order out of the old begins."[44]

Objects of Desire: The Essex House Years

In the Essex House years tableware was the Guild's predominant product. Ashbee wanted his men to produce useful design objects and did not want them to appeal to consumers who bought for the sake of buying. With the exception of jewelry, he forbade his workmen to produce items that were strictly ornamental.[45] Ashbee favored tableware specifically because he knew that consumers were bound to use it, and he truly believed that an object's truth to materials and the visibility of the workman's unique mark would remind consumers that it had been produced under conditions that nurtured man's most innate needs and desires. Ashbee hoped that by using the Guild's objects, consumers' repressed desires for communalism and fine craft would be awakened. "Supply," he wrote, "shall, as far as in me lies, create demand."[46] More importantly, consumers would redirect their money from profit-driven capitalist enterprises to a socialist commune.

Dish with Double Loop Handles (Fig. 1) represents one of the most common tableware items produced by the Guild. The ornamentation is concentrated on the unusually large looped handles and the knob attached to the enameled lid. Ashbee's decision to relegate the ornamentation to these locations was strategic. First, it ensured that the decoration would not be extraneous; the parts of the object most heavily used by consumers would be the most decorative merging ornamentation and utility. Second, the relegation of ornamentation to these spots ensured that the silver body of the vessel would not be overwhelmed by the vessel's decorative elements. The material thus remains exposed as do the marks made by the craftsman's planishing hammer on the surface of the bowl.[47] The bauble on the lid handle is a semiprecious stone; such stones were preferred over gemstones because they lowered the cost of the item and prevented it from seeming pretentious and garish.[48]

A similar strategy is at work in Ashbee's *Butter Knives* (Fig. 2). The intricate decorative wirework of the knife handle is particularly striking, as is the placement of a large semiprecious stone on its handle. Of course, when a consumer used a knife, much of the decoration, including the stone, would be obscured but, because it was integral to the handle, never extraneous. In addition to tableware and flatware, the Guild of Handicraft also produced a series of vessels from what became known as its signature green glass (see plate 39 and Fig. 3). The silver support that cradles the fragile glass container displays most of the object's ornamentation. The metalwork forms a kind of vine or tree pattern that is crowned by a gemstone "bud." Though intricate, this metalwork does not obscure the glass vessel, thus remaining true to Ashbee's goal of leaving materials exposed. The green glass was itself a significant addition to Ashbee's oeuvre. While clearing ground for his home in Chelsea, once the site of a 16th-century inn and affectionately referred to as the Ancient Magpie and Stump, Ashbee unearthed some old green bottle glass.[49] He was inspired to include it in his designs, as it made him feel connected to a past time when, he believed, guilds fostered communal sentiment.

While the Essex House Guild put most of its energy into the production of tableware, it also housed furniture and jewelry workshops. The Guild's furniture designs were in step with those of its tableware; their hallmark features were simplicity and utility.[50] The jewelry produced by the

1
C. R. Ashbee, *Dish with Double Loop Handles* (see plate 44), ca. 1900–01, Guild of Handicraft, silver, enamel, and gemstone. Collection of Crab Tree Farm.

2
C. R. Ashbee, *Butter Knives* (detail of plate 46), ca. 1900, silver with gemstones. Collection of Crab Tree Farm.

3
C. R. Ashbee, *Jar* (see plate 39), ca. 1904, Guild of Handicraft, glass, silver, and gemstone. Collection of Crab Tree Farm.

4–5
C. R. Ashbee, *Necklaces*, ca. 1901, gold and gemstones. Collection of Crab Tree Farm.

Guild of Handicraft was meant to be purely decorative, using semiprecious stones, instead of more precious sapphires and rubies, in the design of necklaces (Figs. 4–5). Inspired by the work of the Florentine goldsmiths, Ashbee believed jewelry was the most visible form of everyday art, and his was meant to serve as an advertisement, on the bosoms of society ladies, for the Guild's social values.[51]

The products of the Essex House Guild generally received favorable reviews in the Victorian design press. In 1897 an anonymous writer from *The Studio* published a review of the Guild:

While the working side of the Guild is assiduously attended to…the social side of the community is not forgotten…. We have dropped by on Wednesday evening and joined Mr. Ashbee at supper with his apprentices. Some of the guildsmen come in after supper, and sometimes an evening is spent in conversation interpolated with songs, catches, and so forth. Indeed, one cannot but think that it is just this quality of human relationship and the efforts of the guildsmen to create a method of life that shall be not merely commercial, which gives to so many of the articles out at Essex House the individual character found in them.[52]

It was, indeed, the best review Ashbee could have hoped for. Whoever wrote the article was able to connect the Guild's lifestyle of anarchic communism and homogenic love—which Ashbee continued to foster outside the workshop with sing-alongs, theater productions, and river trips for his men—to the individual character of its design objects. The system seemed to be working, and buoyed by the Guild's success in the late 1890s, Ashbee took a drastic step and in 1902 moved his workshops and his men to the Cotswold town of Chipping Campden, where he believed that the more direct contact with nature would allow communal and homogenic impulses to blossom to their fullest potential. There, he and his men would truly be able to revolutionize themselves and society.

It is tempting to compare Ashbee's Cotswold enterprise to Carpenter's Millthorpe commune. There are, however, some distinctions between the two that must be brought to the fore. The commune at Millthorpe was explicitly based on Carpenter's principle of homogenic love. The men who joined did so because they possessed a faith in the human need both for platonic comradeship and romantic love with members of the same sex; many became openly involved in sexual relations with their cohabitants. Ashbee's Chipping Campden craftsmen, on the other hand, were not explicitly followers of Carpenter's homogenic belief system. Ashbee believed deeply that homogenic love was a fundamental human desire, but he remained reluctant to publicly expose this belief. When he recruited men into the Guild, he emphasized that he was recruiting craftsmen; he did not intentionally look for or appeal to men who shared his belief in Carpenter's philosophy.

Chipping Campden, when Ashbee and the Guild arrived, was a small provincial town whose streets were still dotted with 15th-century dwellings.[53] Although Ashbee imagined it to be the ideal place for his utopia to finally come to fruition, the Chipping Campden experiment proved to be the end of the Guild of Handicraft. In the beginning, however, the transition from city to country seemed to go quite smoothly. Ashbee's men continued to produce the furniture, tableware, and jewelry that the Guild of Handicraft had become known for. From its inception in East London, the Guild had always offered the public classes in craftwork and now it increased its educational efforts by offering scores of local young men classes in woodwork, enameling, metalwork, and even gardening and exercise through the School of the Guild of Handicraft, which Ashbee had established upon his arrival in the town.[54] His plan was not only to continue to foster homogenic love and anarchic communism among his men but to propagate it. By bringing new recruits into the fold while they were still boys, Ashbee felt that he would really have the chance to educate them in craftwork and engage and develop their desires for homogenic love and communal living. It was his way of ensuring that the physical and mental adaptations the craftsmen had made to their homogenic environment were passed down to the next generation. Ashbee imagined that what began in the Cotswolds would radiate outward, eventually spreading to wider and wider sections of male society.[55]

In his excitement and idealism, however, Ashbee failed to recognize (or simply loathed to acknowledge) how much the Guild of Handicraft depended on the patronage of London's upper crust. It was they, and not the middle classes, who were most inclined to purchase the Guild's products, and at Essex House Ashbee had immediate access to the London art world's exhibitions and publications. In other words, advertising was easy.[56] In the Cotswolds, separated from city life, it was not. Furthermore, Ashbee's conviction that if the Guildsmen simply continued to produce the products they wanted to, "supply shall, as far as in me lies, create demand," was, of course, proven wrong.[57]

Ashbee set out to contest capitalism by integrating Lamarck's theory of adaptation with Carpenter's theory of homogenic love and applying it to his own philosophy of handicraft. By producing design objects communally, the Guildsmen would awaken their repressed desires for homogenic, communal living and would consequently develop and pass on the skills required to sustain such a lifestyle. Although Ashbee's attempt to revolutionize English society was no doubt fruitful for the men who participated in it, the system ultimately failed, in Lamarckian terms, to adapt itself to a changing commodity market that was becoming increasingly driven by the demands of London-based consumers. Isolated in the Cotswolds, Ashbee and his men were no longer in touch with the environment their lifestyle and objects were designed to change. Instead of fostering anticapitalist politics, the return to nature made it impossible for the Guild to adapt to the new demands being created in the city—and as a result it simply could not survive.

C. F. A. Voysey:
An Aesthetic
of Independence and
Interdependence

Zirwat Chowdhury

Between the aesthetics of Christopher Dresser and John Ruskin, it is generally believed no compromise was possible. The former espoused a system of design based upon so-called "art botany," emphasizing science, regularity, repetition, symmetry, and adherence to a regular, natural archetype. The latter proposed that design be based upon the close observation and imitation of nature, believing that imperfections or irregularities were testimony both to the contingencies that shaped the natural environment and the true character of human labor.

Marked by characteristics of symmetry and repetition, the decorations of architect and designer C. F. A. Voysey integrated these divergent approaches. His decorative designs appear to derive primarily from the work of Dresser, but his writings demonstrate a close familiarity with Ruskin. And Voysey's decorative designs show a partial allegiance to Ruskin's philosophy. Voysey's art and thought, in other words, lie somewhere between those of Dresser and Ruskin.

In 1883 Voysey sold his first design pattern to the wallpaper manufacturer Jeffrey & Co., which had produced designs for Morris & Co. Although trained as an architect, Voysey had been introduced to the world of decorative design by his friend, architect and designer Arthur Mackmurdo. Voysey went on to find this component of his work not only lucrative but also intellectually engaging. He produced a large corpus of two- and three-dimensional designs and was a prolific writer, offering a sophisticated account of his own artistic practice and the state of the field.

The concept of order, derived from a singleness of purpose, was central to Voysey's design approach.[1] In his writings, and in his own work as well, the artist advised that forms should not compete with but rather should complement each other, as seen in his design for the wallpaper *Bushey* (Fig. 1).[2]

Voysey's interest in interdependence of forms is not surprising given his associations with Mackmurdo. The two met in the early 1880s, and it was through Mackmurdo's introduction that Voysey made his entry into the world of decorative design.[3] Mackmurdo was the founder of the Century Guild, a craft organization built on principles of collectivism.[4] Collectivism in this form was a political notion applied to artistic collaboration between artists, sculptors, designers, and architects.

Voysey's interests in interdependence, fitness, and collaboration derived not only from Mackmurdo but also from evolutionary thought. In his text *Individuality,* Voysey wrote, "We learn… [of] the interdependence of arts, the laws of construction, and how one form helps principles of another and is delicately related to it."[5]

In 1888, a few years before Voysey began to publish articles on architecture and design, his father—the Reverend Charles Voysey—delivered a lecture at Oxford titled "Some Thoughts on Evolution." In it he accepted Darwinian evolution but cautioned that while Darwin's propositions explained the "why," they did not explain the "how" of the evolutionary process.[6] The answer to how, he argued, lay in the concept of intelligent design as a coefficient of evolution, one in which intelligence served as a kind of "intention" or "interference" interdependent with natural selection.[7] In other words, he claimed that there existed a foundational principle or underlying design of "coordination."[8] C. F. A. Voysey applied a similar idea of coordination to design theory and considered interdependence between architecture and design a necessary element for success. Interde-

C. F. A. Voysey, *Bird, Fruit, Flowers* (detail of plate 36), 1893, watercolor and pencil on paper. Victoria and Albert Museum, London, E.145-1974.

pendence not only needed to exist within a design but also between design and architecture, promoting a correspondence between the building and its furnishings. Voysey often voiced the importance of coordinating the furniture of a home with its architectural space, wallpaper, and textile designs. For example, he said, color, form, and texture should not be "at war" with each other.[9]

Voysey was familiar with the objectives of the Century Guild and agreed with the need for cooperative work between the artistic disciplines, yet maintained a conspicuous distance from the Guild because of its interest in socialist collectivism.[10] Collectivism was contrary to the individualism Voysey advocated. A closer look at Mackmurdo's writing, however, reveals that interdependence was not entirely shadowed by collectivism, explaining in part why the two designers had so many affinities. In the preface to *Pressing Questions*, written more than two decades after the founding of the Century Guild, Mackmurdo stated:

Economics merely demand that the activity of each individual shall be of a measure that shall secure the best results for the individual. Ethics require that this activity be of a kind that shall promote or favour the opportunity of others…. Religion then must forever be the basis and the stay of society. Religion, and religion alone, can cure the social body of its ills. By religion we mean the sympathetic imagination which alone can control and ennoble conduct…[11]

Even though Mackmurdo's ideas developed into more extensive notions of profit sharing, the heart of his argument was built upon Ruskin's ethics, which Voysey himself explicitly acknowledged and supported in his *Reason as a Basis of Art*.[12] Mackmurdo, moreover, is credited with having introduced Voysey to Ruskin's work. Indeed, foregrounding Mackmurdo's Ruskinian tendencies are his inclusion of excerpts from Ruskin's *Time and Tide* in *Pressing Questions*:

The healthy sense of progress, which is necessary to the strength and happiness of men, does not consist in the anxiety of a struggle to attain higher place or rank but in gradually perfecting the manner and accomplishing the ends of the life which we have chosen, or which circumstances have determined for us…[13]

The citation Mackmurdo chose to include, with its reference to the "anxiety of a struggle," suggests both Ruskin's and Voysey's unease with Darwinian and Spencerian notions of "survival of the fittest." The chief governing sentiments for Ruskin and his followers were cooperation and empathy for one's fellow beings, as well as satisfaction with one's rank in society. Ruskin went on to argue in this passage that excessive wealth gained by one person can only lead to a loss for others. He proposes, therefore, that limits should be set on individual wealth so that the upper classes can dedicate their energies not to accumulating wealth but to advancing life.[14] In other words, he argues against the Spencerian tendencies of competition in society and speaks in favor of a counter model where cooperation or interdependence foster better workmanship and a higher standard of living for all. Ruskin and Mackmurdo argue that in a more egalitarian society the workman can strive to develop his own craft rather than satisfy the need to become master of the whole production process.[15]

Pleasure in workmanship, in fact, is the driving principle behind Voysey's well-known essay "Ideas in Things." In the essay he proposed a correspondence between the pleasure with which a workman produces an object and the pleasure a viewer or owner derives from an object.[16] Although not nearly as critical of industrial manufactures as William Morris, Voysey was opposed to a production process that denied individual thought and creativity. He was, instead, in favor of making work more pleasurable, lauding designers like Mackmurdo who embraced the labor-saving capability of machines to create straight and simple forms.[17] Indeed, Voysey's design aesthetic encouraged the use of bright and pure colors and sinuous lines; angularity was to be avoided, in order—as Voysey saw it—to provide repose for its viewers.[18] *Bushey*, for example, presents a repeated plant form with orange flowers and green leaves juxtaposed with the yellow stems.[19] The symmetry and careful spacing of each leaf and flower are unlike the busier and activist compositional strategy that appears in Morris's work from the 1870s and 1880s (see plate 20).[20]

Even though Voysey had likely ventured into the design profession out of economic necessity, he molded his design practice in accordance with his artistic philosophy. In "The Aims and Conditions of the Modern Decorator" he argued (like Dresser before him) that flatness in designs was to be lauded because denying naturalism offered a designer more channels for creativity.[21] Indeed, his writings frequently voice opposition to mimetic practice. Instead of copying nature, artists must bring their individual subjectivity to representation through the process of selection and analysis. Similarly, he was critical of "stylisms" and the dependence of artists and architects on stylistic movements rather than on practicality, utility, and structure.

Voysey argued that the strength of the Gothic style rested on its being not just a "convention" but a "principle"—one that forged a "system of designing from within outwards."[22] Following the influential British designer A. W. Pugin, who looked to the Gothic period, Voysey advocated fitness, which he defined as "a divine law, and by fitness we mean not only material suitability but moral fitness—that which expresses our best thoughts and feelings and our purest moral sense."[23] Voysey's essay "1874 and After" provided one of the clearest examples of the designer's engagement with the concepts—key to evolutionary thought—of fitness, utility, and materialism. While critical of the excessive materialism of his time, he nonetheless recognized that it was the materialism of science that liberated design from blind subservience to classicism. He says:

We must remember that this Revolt against styleism [*sic*] and pursuit of utilitarianism was in the womb years before and was the child of Science and the Prince Consort. The 1851 Exhibition awakened the idea of utility as the basis of Art. All that was necessary for daily life could be, and ought to be, made beautiful.[24]

Later in the same essay he lamented that the market was too competitive to foster imaginative work, adding that if a businessman understood that "beauty was as needful to his moral and spiritual well-being as it is to any other kind of worker," then he would be satisfied with it more than with monetary profit.[25] In his 1906 essay *Reason as a Basis of Art*, Voysey urged readers to

1

C. F. A. Voysey, *Bushey*, (wallpaper design), Essex & Co., ca. 1890, color wash on paper. RIBA Library Drawings & Archives Collections, SB117/Voy [661].

"cultivate deep reverence and live for something higher and better than ourselves...to fix the mind on human qualities rather than the person" in order to encourage a shift from materialism to idealism.[26]

Voysey's disdain for the excessive materialism of contemporary society emerged in most of his essays. In "Ideas in Things," for example, he called materialism the "demon of unrighteousness."[27] His design principles were thus an amalgamation of Dresser's and Ruskin's propositions: While believing in the need for individuality, he argued that a capacity for sympathy was inherent to human beings.

But as much as he supported the Ruskinian ideal of interdependence and sympathy, Voysey also valued individuality, which he saw as an agent of modernity and productivity.[28] Scholars on Voysey have argued that his embrace of individuality may have stemmed from his witnessing at an early age his father's excommunication from the Church of England.[29] In *Individuality* he argued that individuality produced friction, which in turn produced heat, which ultimately produced force.[30] In "1874 and After" he argued that the Gothic style, with its angularity and lightning-like forms, represented conflict, but a kind that creates "aspiration" and "movement."[31] In fact, Voysey's 1889 design *The Demon* (Fig. 2), which represents gargoyle-like creatures caught in flames that mirror the curves of their arms and wings, would seem to contradict his propositions about designs that provide repose to their viewers. He contained the seeming excess of the design's ornate motifs within the symmetry of its composition, however, and softened its angularity with the mirroring curvilinear patterns. Voysey thus created a composition that not only stimulates the viewer but also manages to contain the busy pattern within an organized framework. Similar to the *Demon*, the bodies of the water snakes resonate with the curvilinear contours of the seaweed surrounding them in *Snakes among Weed* (Fig. 3). The eye of the snake seems to be tamed by the harmony between its form and its environment, by the undulating motion of its body and that of the grass around it, and by the softening effects of the cool blue and green. While Voysey wanted his designs to provide repose to their viewers, it is useful to recall his interest in the spiritual growth of his clients. For Voysey, repose did not have to be concomitant with luxury. This association, he believed, was one of the shortcomings of classical motifs.[32] He further argued that conformity was a sign of laziness and collectivism a sign of passivity.[33]

Voysey's use of repeated plant forms and symmetry may align his work with the design theories of Dresser, but his interest in interdependence reveals his indebtedness to the work of Ruskin. However, Voysey's interests in individuality distance him from the collectivist principles of Ruskin, Morris, and Mackmurdo and place his ideas alongside, once again, those of Dresser. While the debates between Ruskin and Dresser may have set their design theories in opposition, Voysey's oeuvre provides an example of a more inclusive space of late 19th-century British design practice.

2
C. F. A. Voysey, *Demon* (tile),
ca. 1890, ceramic. Collection
of Crab Tree Farm.

3
C. F. A. Voysey, *Snakes
among Weed*, (wallpaper
design), ca. 1896, color wash
on paper. RIBA Library
Drawings & Archives Collections, SB117/Voy [673].

Design in the Age of Darwin:
From William Morris to Frank Lloyd Wright
Stephen F. Eisenman

1. Thomas Huxley Papers, Imperial College of Science and Technology, London, cited in Adrian Desmond and James Moore, *Darwin* (London: Penguin Books, 1991), 497.

2. Public Acts of the State of Tennessee Passed by the Sixty-fourth General Assembly, 1925, chapter no. 27, House bill no. 185.

3. The events are represented in the 1955 play *Inherit the Wind* by Jerome Lawrence and Robert Edwin Lee. In the well-known film version (1960), Spencer Tracy played Henry Drummond, the character based on Clarence Darrow, and Fredric March played Matthew Harrison Brady, the character based on William Jennings Bryan.

4. In the United States District Court for the Middle District of Pennsylvania, *Kitzmiller, et al. v. Dover Area School District, et al.,* 400 F. Supp. 2d 707 (M.D. Pa. 2005).

5. Oliver J. Thatcher, ed., *The Early Medieval World,* vol. 5, *The Library of Original Sources* (Milwaukee: University Research Extension Co., 1907), 363.

6. This particular proposition became very well known in the 19th century and was even illustrated by James Paxton for a new American edition: William Paley, *Natural Theology* (Boston: Lincoln and Edmands, 1829), 14.

7. Jonathan Smith, *Charles Darwin and Victorian Visual Culture* (Cambridge: Cambridge University Press, 2006), 185.

8. Samuel Wilberforce, "Darwin's Origin of Species," *Quarterly Review* 102 (1860): 225–64.

9. Charles Darwin, *The Origin of Species by Means of Natural Selection, or, The Preservation of Favoured Races in the Struggle for Life* (1859) (London: J. Murray, 1902), 403.

10. Robert M. Young, "Darwin's Metaphor," in *Darwin's Metaphor: Nature's Place in Victorian Culture* (Cambridge: Cambridge University Press, 1985), passim.

11. Stephen J. Gould, *The Structure of Evolutionary Theory* (Cambridge, MA: Belknap Press, 2002), 121.

12. Charles Bell, *The Anatomy and Philosophy of Expression, as Connected with the Fine Arts* (London: George Bell and Sons, 1904), 174

13. M. Digby Wyatt, "An Attempt to Define the Principles which should determine Form in the Decorative Arts," in *Lectures on the Results of the Great Exhibition of 1851 Delivered before the Society of Arts, Manufacturers, and Commerce at the Suggestion of Prince Albert, President of the Society,* vol. 1 (London: David Bogue, 1852), 215.

14. Robert W. Duemling, review of *Matthew Digby Wyatt* by Nicholas Pevsner, *Art Bulletin* 34, no. 4 (December 1952): 326.

15. Horatio Greenough, *Form and Function: Remarks on Art, Design and Architecture,* ed. H. A. Small (Berkeley and Los Angeles: University of California Press, 1958), 58, cited in Philip Steadman, *The Evolution of Designs* (Cambridge: Cambridge University Press, 1979), 58.

16. C. F. A. Voysey, "Ideas in Things," in *The Arts Connected with Building,* ed. T. Raffles Davison (London: B. T. Batsford, 1909), 110.

17. Peter Collins, "The Biological Analogy," in *Changing Ideals in Modern Architecture: 1750–1950* (Montreal: McGill/Queens, 1967), 149–58.

18. Augustus Welby Pugin, *Contrasts, or, A Parallel Between the Noble Edifices of the Middle Ages and Corresponding Buildings of the Present Day* (London: Charles Dolman, 1841), 1.

19. Ibid., 5.

20. John Ruskin, "Lectures on Art," *The Complete Works of John Ruskin,* vol. xiv (New York: Thomas Y. Crowell and Co., n.d.), 19.

21. John Ruskin, "The Deteriorative Power of Conventional Art over Nations," in *The Two Paths* (London: Smith, Elder and Co., 1859), 1–54.

22. Geoffrey Scott, *The Architecture of Humanism—A Study in the History of Taste* (London: Constable and Company, 1914), 165.

23. Ibid, 168–69.

24. E. E. Viollet-le-Duc, "Style," in *Dictionnaire Raisonné de l'Architecture Française du XIe au XVIe Siècle* (Paris: A. Morel, 1854–68), 8:145, cited in Steadman, 73.

25. James Fergusson, *An Historical Inquiry into the True Principles of Beauty in Art, especially with Reference to Architecture* (London: Longman, Brown and Green, 1849), section 4, 156, cited in Steadman, 83. Also see these extraordinary articles by David Brett: "The Interpretation of Ornament," *Journal of Design History* 1, no. 2 (1988): 103–11, and "Design Reform and the Laws of Nature," *Design Issues* 11, no. 3 (1995): 37–49. In addition see Barbara Whitney Keyser, "Ornament as Idea: Indirect Imitation of Nature in the Design Reform Movement," *Journal of Design History* 11, no. 2 (1998): 127–44.

26. James Fergusson, *History of Indian and Eastern Architecture* (London: John Murray, 1876); Thomas Huxley, *Life and Letters of Thomas Henry Huxley* (London: Macmillan, 1900), 1, 231, cited in Desmond and Moore, 560; Partha Mitter, *Indian Art* (Oxford: Oxford University Press, 2001), 20.

27. Gottfried Semper, "Development of Architectural Style," *Inland Architect and News Record* 14, no. 7 (1889): 76, cited in Steadman, 73.

28. Ibid. Also cited in Gottfried Semper, *Style in the Technical and Tectonic Arts,* trans. Harry Francis Mallgrave and Michael Robinson (Los Angeles: Getty Trust Publications, Getty Research Institute, 2004), 57.

29. J. Mordaunt Crook, "Design and Practice in British Architecture: Studies in Architectural History Presented to Howard Colvin," *Architectural History* 27 (1984): 555–78. Also see Alberto Perez-Gomez, *Architecture and the Crisis of Modern Science* (Cambridge, MA: MIT Press, 1983).

30. Darwin, 63.

31. Harry Braverman, *Labor and Monopoly Capital: The Degradation of Work in the Twentieth Century* (New York: Monthly Review Press), 1974.

32. Adrian Desmond, *The Politics of Evolution: Morphology, Medicine and Reform in Radical London* (Chicago and London: University of Chicago Press), 1989.

33. Owen Jones, *The Grammar of Ornament* (London: Bernard Quaritch, 1910), 1.

34. Burne-Jones Papers, Fitzwilliam Museum, Cambridge, xxiii–13, cited in *William Morris,* ed. Linda Parry (New York: Harry Abrams, 1996), 162.

35. Darwin, 168, cited in Gould, 251–52.

36. Also see the similar illustrations in Richard Owens, *On the Nature of Limbs* (London: John Van Voorst, 1849), pl. ii.

37. J. W. von Goethe, *The Metamorphosis of Plants* (Kimberton, PA: Bio-Dynamic Farming Association, 1993), 53.

38. B. Mueller and C. J. Engard, *Goethe's Botanical Writings* (Honolulu: University of Hawaii Press, 1952), 14, cited in Gould, 285.

39. Larry D. Lutchmansingh, "Evolutionary Affinity in Arthur Mackmurdo's Botanical Design," *Design Issues* 6, no. 2 (Spring 1990): 51–57.

40. William Morris, *The Collected Works of William Morris* (London: Longmans, Green and Co., 1914), 22:xii. The original Ruskin is likely to have been the following: "But the transformations believed in by the anatomists are as yet proved true in no single instance, spiritual or material; and I cannot so often, or too earnestly urge you not to waste your time in guessing what animals may once have been, while you remain in ignorance of what they are." (John Ruskin, *The Complete Works of John Ruskin*, ed. E. T. Cook and A. Wedderburn (London: George Allen, 1903–12), xxv, 57.

41. William Morris, *The Collected Letters of William Morris*, ed. Norman Kelvin (Princeton: Princeton University Press, 1987), 2:328.

42. Stephen F. Eisenman, "Communism in Furs: A Dream of Prehistory in William Morris's *John Ball*," *Art Bulletin* 87, no. 1 (March 2005): 92–110.

43. William Morris and Belfort E. Bax, *Socialism: Its Growth and Outcome* (London: Macmillan, 1893), 20.

44. Charles Darwin and Alfred Wallace, "On the Tendency of Species to Form Varieties; and on the Perpetuation of Varieties and Species by Natural Means of Selection," in *Journal of the Proceedings of the Linnean Society* (London: Longman, Brown and Green, 1858), 3:45–62; Christopher Dresser, "Contributions to Organographic Botany," in *Journal of the Proceedings of the Linnean Society* (London: Longman, Brown and Green, 1858), 3:148–50. Information concerning Dresser's nonattendance was kindly supplied by Gina Douglas, librarian and archivist, Linnean Society of London.

45. Christopher Dresser, "Stem and Leaf and their Transmutation," *The Register of Facts and Occurrences Relating to Literature, the Sciences and the Arts,* August 1860, 39–45. Dresser's articles on plant morphology commenced in July 1861. My thanks to Stuart Durant for his great generosity in sending me photocopies of these articles. See his "Christopher Dresser and the Use of Contemporary Science," *Decorative Arts Society Journal* 29 (2005): 23–29.

46. Christopher Dresser, "Stem and Leaf," 41.

47. Richard Owen, *On the Anatomy of Vertebrates* (London: Longmans, Green and Co., 1866), 1:v–vi.

48. Cited in Desmond and Moore, *Darwin*, 452.

49. Richard Owen, *On the Nature of Limbs*, 2.

50. Darwin, 434, cited in Gould, 316.

51. Owen, *On the Nature of Limbs*, 119, cited in Gould, 317.

52. Owen, *On the Nature of Limbs,* 15; Michael Whiteway, ed., *Shock of the Old: Christopher Dresser's Design Revolution* (New York: Harry N. Abrams, 2004), 50.

53. Gottfried Semper, *The Four Elements of Architecture and Other Writings* (Cambridge: Cambridge University Press, 1989), 22.

54. Christopher Dresser, *Unity in Variety*, (London: James S. Virtue, 1860), xiv.

55. Ibid.

56. Samuel Wilberforce, "On 'The Origin of Species,'" in *Quarterly Review* 108 (1860): 259.

57. *Lectures on the Results of the Great Exhibition of 1851 delivered before the Society of Arts, Manufacturers, and Commerce*, vol. 2 (London: David Bogue, 1852), 216.

58. Christopher Dresser, *The Principles of Decorative Design* (London, Paris, and New York: Cassell, Petter and Galpin, n.d. [1873]), 4.

59. John Ruskin, *The Two Paths,* 10.

60. Ibid., 14–15.

61. Christopher Dresser, *Popular Manual of Botany* (Edinburgh: Adam and Charles Black, 1860), 29.

62. Ruskin, *The Two Paths*, 110.

63. Christopher Dresser, *The Art of Decorative Design* (London: Day and Son, 1862), 164.

64. Christopher Dresser, *Principles*, 21.

65. Edward B. Tylor, *Primitive Culture* (London: John Murray, 1871), 60–61.

66. Dresser, *The Art of Decorative Design*, 82–83.

67. Robert Twombly and Narciso G. Menocal, *Louis Sullivan: The Poetry of Architecture* (New York and London: W. W. Norton, 2000), 73.

68. Frank Lloyd Wright, *Frank Lloyd Wright—Collected Writings*, ed. Bruce Brooks Pfeiffer (New York: Rizzoli Books, 1992), 1:90.

69. Oscar Wilde, *The Soul of Man under Socialism* (Boston: John W. Luce and Co., n.d.), passim.

70. Voysey, 130.

71. Herbert Spencer, *First Principles* (1862) (London: Williams and Norgate, 1911), 132, cited in Valerie A. Haines, "Is Spencer's Theory an Evolutionary Theory?," *American Journal of Sociology* 93, no. 5 (1988): 1202.

72. C. R. Ashbee, *American Sheaves and English Seed Corn* (London: Essex House Press, 1901), 107–08.

73. Frank Lloyd Wright, "The Art and Craft of the Machine," in *Frank Lloyd Wright: Writings and Buildings,* ed. Edgar Kaufmann and Ben Raeburn (New York and Scarborough, Ontario: New American Library, 1974), 55–73.

74. C. R. Ashbee, *Where the Great City Stands—A Study in the New Civics* (London: Essex House Press and B. T. Batsford, 1917), 20–21.

Louis Sullivan, Herbert Spencer, and the Medium of Architecture
David Van Zanten

1. On Sullivan's theory: Sherman Paul, *Louis Sullivan: An Architect in American Thought* (Englewood, NJ: Prentice-Hall, 1962); Narciso Menocal, *Architecture as Nature: The Transcendentalist Idea of Louis Sullivan* (Madison, WI: University of Wisconsin Press, 1981); Lauren Weingarden, *Louis H. Sullivan and a Nineteenth-Century Discourse on the Poetics of Architecture* (London: Ashgate Press, forthcoming); Lauren S. Weingarden, "Louis Sullivan's Ornament and the Poetics of Architecture," in John Zukowsky, ed., *Chicago Architecture, 1872–1922* (Munich: Prestel, 1987), 229–50. Vincent Scully draws a general analysis of Sullivan's work from "Louis Sullivan's Architectural Ornament," *Perspecta* 5, (1959), 73–80. By Sullivan: *The Autobiography of an Idea* (Washington: AIA Press, 1924) and Sullivan's shorter writings: Robert Twombly, ed., *Louis Sullivan: The Public Papers* (Chicago: University of Chicago Press, 1988). On Sullivan: Hugh Morrison, *Louis Sullivan: Prophet of Modern Architecture,* 1935, 2nd edition by Timothy Samuelson (New York: W. W. Norton, 1998); Robert Twombly, *Louis Sullivan: His Life and Work* (New York: Viking, 1986); Narciso Menocal and Robert Twombly, *Louis Sullivan: The Poetry of Architecture* (New York: W. W. Norton, 2000).

2. He also adored the music of Richard Wagner and Michelangelo's frescoes in the Sistine Chapel. Just what did Sullivan read? His confidence to the *Daily Inter-Ocean* reporter was unusual. Frank Lloyd Wright remembers in his *Autobiography*, "He adored Whitman, as I did. And, explain it however you can, [he] was deep in Herbert Spencer. He gave Spencer's *Synthetic Philosophy* to me to take home and read." *Frank Lloyd Wright, An Autobiography* (New York: Duell, Sloan and Pearce, 1943), 103. In 1949, in his *Genius and the Mobocracy* (New York: Duell, Sloan and Pearce, 1949), Wright wrote, "As for [Sullivan's] literary 'tastes,' he loved Whitman's *Leaves of Grass* and read Herbert Spencer. Early in my life he gave me Spencer and Whitman to read. Not so strange a pair to draw to as one

might think," 56. In his *Autobiography of an Idea* (1924), Sullivan cites Taine, Trautwein's *Engineer's Pocket Book,* and the naturalist Asa Gray's visits to his classes at Boston English High School. The 1909 auction catalog of his extensive library survives at the Art Institute of Chicago, recording his possession of Swinburne, Max Muller, Goethe's *Werke* (what good did that do him in German?), Kipling, Molière, and Kock—but that was what he was willing to sell. The more personal library in his Gulf house survived down to Hurricane Katrina with his annotated copy of Whitman's *Leaves of Grass.*

3. See the most recent study: Mark Francis, *Herbert Spencer and The Invention of Modern Life* (Ithaca: Cornell, 2007), part III, chapter 13, "The Meaning of Life."

4. On Hooley's Theatre, see Charles E. Gregerson, *Dankmar Adler: His Theatres and Auditoriums* (Athens, OH: Ohio University Press, 1990), 56. I have tried to trace Sullivan's French parallels: "Sullivan to 1890," Wim de Wit, ed., *Louis Sullivan: The Function of Ornament* (New York: W. W. Norton, 1986), 13–63; David Van Zanten, *Sullivan's City: The Meaning of Ornament for Louis Sullivan* (New York: W. W. Norton, 2000).

5. See the introduction to his *Flore ornemental* (Paris: Dunod, 1866–76) citing Viollet-le-Duc's entry "flore" in his *Dictionnaire raisonné* (vol. 5, 485–524, Paris: Bance, 1861). Ruprich-Robert succeeded Viollet-le-Duc as professor of *composition d'ornement* in 1851 at the Ecole des Arts Décoratifs, across the street from which Sullivan lived while a student in Paris in 1874–75. His copies of Ruprich-Robert's plates are in the collection of the Art Institute of Chicago.

6. See Donald D. Egbert and Paul E. Sprague, "In Search of John Edelmann," *A. I. A. Journal* (February 1966), 35–41. Doodling floral efflorescences seems to have filled Edelmann's idle moments: Irving K. Pond, MS, *Autobiography of Irving K. Pond*, in the American Academy of Arts and Letters, New York, chapter 8.

7. "Essay on Inspiration," *Inland Architect and News Record* VIII (December 1886), 61–64; republished in Twombly, *Louis Sullivan: The Public Papers,* 10–28; the French MS "Etude sur l'Inspiration" is in the Art Institute of Chicago and has been published in English translation by Twombly and Menocal, *Louis Sullivan: The Poetry of Architecture,* 161–70; and in the original French in David Van Zanten, "Etude sur l'inspiration," *EAV* 12 (2006/2007): 46–61.

8. Or the mysterious opera house facade shown at the Chicago Architectural Club in 1913 and reproduced in their catalogue.

9. Paul Sprague, *The Drawings of Louis Henry Sullivan* (Princeton: Princeton University Press, 1979). See plates 33–34. Wright gave the drawings to the Avery Architectural and Fine Arts Library.

10. Frank Lloyd Wright, "Louis Sullivan—his Work," *Architectural Record* 56 (July 1924), 28–32, especially 29–30. Twenty-five years later he wrote of this moment, "As he threw [on my desk] the 'sketch' with the first bays outlined in pencil upon it, I sensed what had happened…. In his vision, here beyond doubt, was the dawn of a new day in skyscraper design." *Genius and the Mobocracy,* 59.

11. I explore this further in my essay "The Nineteenth Century: The Projecting of Chicago as a Commercial City and the Rationalization of Design and Construction," in John Zukowsky, ed., *Chicago and New York: Architectural Interactions* (Chicago: Art Institute of Chicago, 1984), 30–48. Daniel Bluestone takes it further: *Constructing Chicago* (New Haven: Yale University Press, 1991), especially chapter 4. This alienation in American cultural production is treated more broadly in Michael

T. Gilmore, *American Romanticism and the Marketplace* (Chicago: University of Chicago Press, 1985).

12. *Léonard, maçon de la Creuse* (Paris: Maspero, 1976), 189–90.

13. Lauren Weingarden, *Louis Sulllivan and a Nineteenth-Century Discourse on the Poetics of Architecture.*

14. The issue of an "impressionist" interpretation of early Chicago skyscraper design is developed by Joanna Merwood Salisbury in her forthcoming book on John Wellborn Root from University of Chicago Press.

15. Frank Lloyd Wright, *Frank Lloyd Wright: Writings and Buildings,* ed. Edgar Kaufmann and Ben Raeburn (New York: Meridian, 1960), 73.

16. Lloyd Engelbrecht, "Adler & Sullivan's Pueblo Opera House: City Status for a New Town in the Rockies," *Art Bulletin* 67, no. 2 (June 1985), 277–95. Sullivan's newspaper interview is not quoted there, however.

17. William Jordy, "The Tall Buildings," in de Wit, *Louis Sullivan: The Function of Ornament,* 65–157.

18. A mass of research is underway and further line of argument underlies this statement. Noting Sullivan's formative contact with Viollet-le-Duc and his follower Ruprich-Robert at the Ecole des Arts Décoratifs, let me cite one pamphlet by Viollet-le-Duc from that moment, putting forward ornament as the model for creative design: *Union Centrale des arts décoratifs appliqués a l'industrie; Conférence de M. Viollet-le-Duc sur l'enseignement des arts du dessin,* n.d. [c. 1875].

19. There also survive Sullivan's pencil design drawings for an alternative facade configuration for his last bank in Columbus, Wisconsin, of 1919. The drawings are now in the Avery Architectural and Fine Arts Library at Columbia University, and published in Lauren Weingarden, *Louis Sullivan: The Banks* (Cambridge, MA: MIT Press, 1987), 124–41.

20. *Chicago Graphic,* December 19, 1891.

21. Sullivan, *Autobiography of an Idea,* 297–98.

22. Neil Levine, "The Quadruple Block Plan and Frank Lloyd Wright's Obsession with the Grid," *EAV* 11 (2005/2006), 62–83. This is part of a larger argument soon to appear as a book.

23. Understood as nature commodified following William Cronon's *Nature's Metropolis* (New York: W. W. Norton, 1991).

24. Frank Lloyd Wright, "In the Cause of Architecture: V. The Meaning of Materials – the Kiln," *Architectural Record* (January 1929): 555–61, especially page 560. It is worthwhile to quote Wright's whole evocation: "The only limit to Sullivan's treatment was the degree to which the substance of the pliable clay would stay up between the thumb and finger and come through the fire. Background disappeared but surface was preserved. There was no background, as such, anywhere. All was of the surface, out of material. So no sense of ornament *applied* [Wright's emphasis] to Terra-Cotta, because Terra-Cotta became ornament and ornament itself."

25. *Architectural Record,* 1924, 29: "As to materials, the grasp of the Master's imagination gripped them all pretty much alike. As to relying upon them for beauties of their own, he had no need — no patience. They were stuff to bear the stamp of his imagination and bear it they did, cast iron, wrought iron, marble, plaster, concrete, wood."

26. I heard these words used by "Beaux-Arts"–trained architects in the 1950s and 1960s in New York.

27. Both the presentation drawing and the working drawings are in the collection of the Block Museum of Art, Northwestern University.

28. "Frank Lloyd Wright," *Frankfurter Zeitung,* June 30, 1931. Behrendt continued to refine this analysis in his

Modern Building (New York: Harcourt Brace, 1937) and in his unpublished catalogue essay of 1941 for the Museum of Modern Art's Wright exhibition: Peter Reed, William Kaizen, and Kathryn Smith, *The Show to End All Shows* (New York: Museum of Modern Art, 2004), 116–33.

29. This was the publication of his 1938–39 Charles Eliot Norton lectures at Harvard University. Reto Geiser is finishing a dissertation on Giedion at the ETH, Zurich, and has been kind in sharing information with me.

30. Perhaps the most famous of these was the Anglo-Argentine W. H. Hudson, publishing his evocative *Purple Land* of 1885, his utopian *A Crystal Age* in 1887, his immensely popular *Green Mansions* in 1904, and his autobiographical *Far Away and Long Ago* in 1918. Guiraldes virtually created the gaucho with his *Don Segundo Sombra,* 1926.

31. See Anthony Alofsin, *Frank Lloyd Wright, The Lost Years, 1910–1922* (Chicago: University of Chicago Press, 1993); Kevin Nute, *Frank Lloyd Wright and Japan* (London and New York: Routledge, 1993); Julia Meech, *Frank Lloyd Wright and the Art of Japan* (New York: Abrams, 2001). On the Griffins, see Paul Kruty and Paul Sprague, *Two American Architects in India: Walter B. Griffin and Marion M. Griffin, 1935–1937* (Urbana-Champaign: School of Architecture, University of Illinois, 1997); Meredith Walker, Adrienne Kabos, James Weirick, *Building for Nature: Walter Burley Griffin and Castlecrag* (Castlecrag: Walter Burley Griffin Society, 1994).

32. See Heidi Kief-Niederwöhrmeier, *Frank Lloyd Wright und Europa* (Stuttgart: K. Krämer, 1983); Anthony Alofsin, ed., *Frank Lloyd Wright: Europe and Beyond, 1910–1922* (Berkeley, CA: University of California Press, 1999).

Designing Evolution: Darwin's Illustrations
Jacob W. Lewis

1. Charles Darwin, *On the Origin of Species by Means of Natural Selection, or, The Preservation of Favoured Races in the Struggle for Life* (London: J. Murray, 1859), 116–17.

2. Jonathan Smith, *Charles Darwin and Victorian Visual Culture* (Cambridge: Cambridge University Press, 2006), 1.

3. John Lindley, *The Vegetable Kingdom: Or, The Structure, Classification, and Uses of Plants, Illustrated Upon the Natural System* (London: Bradbury and Evans, 1846). See Charles Darwin, *On the Various Contrivances by Which British and Foreign Orchids Are Fertilised by Insects, and on the Good Effects of Intercrossing* (London: J. Murray, 1862), 174.

4. Charles Darwin, *The Correspondence of Charles Darwin*, vol. 8 (London and New York: Cambridge University Press, 1985), 345–47.

5. Darwin, "The Origin of Species (1859)," in *Darwin*, ed. Philip Appleman (New York and London: W. W. Norton, 2001), 135.

6. See Barbara Whitney Keyser, "Ornament as Idea: Indirect Imitation of Nature in the Design Reform Movement," *Journal of Design History* 11, no. 2 (1998): 127–44.

7. Richard Redgrave, *Manual of Design, Compiled from the Writings and Addresses of Richard Redgrave* (New York: Scribner, Welford, & Armstrong, 1876), 23–26.

8. David Brett, "Design Reform and the Laws of Nature," *Design Issues* 11, no. 3 (Autumn 1995): 39–40.

9. Christopher Dresser, "Botany as Adapted to the Arts and Art Manufactures," *Art Journal* (December 1, 1858): 362.

10. Smith, 155.

11. Ibid., 151.

12. Christopher Dresser, *Principles of Victorian Decorative Design* (1873; reprint, New York: Dover, 1995), 97.

13. Dresser, "Botany as Adapted to the Arts and Art Manufactures," 362.

14. John Ruskin, *Proserpina: Studies of Wayside Flowers, while the air was yet pure among the Alps, and in the Scotland and England which my father knew,* vol. 2 (Sunnyside, Orpington, Kent: G. Allen, 1882), 6.

15. Smith, 29.

16. Ruskin held a synchronic understanding of nature, meaning he favored the variety of life in the present without attention to its development. Darwin, on the other hand, viewed the present natural world as the result of diachronic forces, that is, the result of changes over time.

17. Charles Darwin, *The Movement and Habits of Climbing Plants* (London: Murray, 1875), 149.

18. Darwin, "The Origin of Species (1859)," 134–35.

19. The book outlines three principles of development: "serviceable habits," where expressions of desire or need become physiological habit through repeated performance; "antithesis," where contrasting bodily expressions communicate opposite emotions, thus making expression more legible between members of a species; finally, "the direct action of the nervous system," where certain emotions are products of physiological reactions, largely independent of will and habit. See Charles Darwin, *The Expression of the Emotions in Man and Animals*, with an Introduction, Afterword and Commentaries by Paul Ekman (New York and Oxford: Oxford University Press, 1998), 34.

20. Charles Bell, *The Anatomy and Philosophy of Expression as Connected with the Fine Arts*, 3rd ed. (London: Murray, 1844). For a general history of Bell's text, see Frederick Cummings, "Charles Bell and the Anatomy of Expression," *Art Bulletin* 46, no. 2 (June 1964): 191–203. For an analysis of Darwin's views on Bell, see Smith, 186–98. For a study of Darwin's arguments against an aesthetic understanding of expression, and its relation to the work of Walter Benjamin, see Susan Buck-Morss, "Aesthetics and Anaesthetics: Walter Benjamin's Artwork Essay Reconsidered," *October* 62 (Autumn 1992): 3–41.

21. Darwin, *The Expression of the Emotions in Man and Animals*, 21.

22. T. S. Baynes, "Darwin on Expression (Review)," *Edinburgh Review* 137 (April 1873): 516. This passage is discussed in Smith, 23–24.

23. Baynes, "Darwin on Expression (Review)," 521.

24. Darwin, *The Expression of the Emotions in Man and Animals*, 19.

25. Phillip Prodger, "Photography and the Expression of the Emotions," in Charles Darwin, *The Expression of the Emotions in Man and Animals,* Paul Ekman, ed. (New York: Oxford University Press, 1998), 404.

26. Prodger, "Photography and the Expression of the Emotions," 407.

27. See Stephanie Spencer, "O. G. Rejlander: Art Studies," in *British Photography in the Nineteenth Century: The Fine Art Tradition*, ed. Mike Weaver (Cambridge and New York: Cambridge University Press, 1989).

28. Darwin, *The Expression of the Emotions in Man and Animals*, 147.

29. Walter Benjamin, "Little History of Photography," in *Walter Benjamin: Selected Writings*, ed. Michael W. Jennings, Howard Eiland, and Gary Smith (Cambridge, MA, and London: Belknap Press of Harvard University Press, 1999), 510.

30. In its first edition, Charles Darwin, *The Expression of the Emotions in Man and Animals*, 148–49, plate I, figure 1.

31. Phillip Prodger, "Rejlander, Darwin, and the Evolution of 'Ginx's Baby,'" *History of Photography* 23, no. 3 (Autumn 1999): 265, figure 5A.

32. Edward Jenkins, *Ginx's Baby: His Birth and Other Misfortunes. A Satire.* (Boston: J. R. Osgood & Co., 1871). See Prodger, "Rejlander, Darwin, and the Evolution of 'Ginx's Baby'"

33. Prodger, "Rejlander, Darwin, and the Evolution of 'Ginx's Baby,'" 261.

34. "The Expression of Emotions in Man and Animals, by Charles Darwin (Review)," *The Athenaeum*, no. 2351 (November 16, 1872): 632. See also Smith, 229.

35. For more on the use of photography as scientific evidence, and the skepticism of 19th-century viewers, see Jennifer Tucker, *Nature Exposed: Photography as Eyewitness in Victorian Science* (Baltimore: Johns Hopkins University Press, 2005).

36. Adrien Tournachon and G. B. Duchenne du Boulogne, *Fright*, salted paper print, ca. 1854; first published in G.-B. Duchenne, *Mécanisme de la physionomie humaine, ou, analyse électro-physiologique de l'expression des passions* (Paris: Renouard, 1862).

37. Carol Armstrong, *Scene in a Library: Reading the Photograph in the Book, 1843–1875* (Cambridge, MA, and London: MIT Press, 1998), 105.

38. Ruskin, *Proserpina: Studies of Wayside Flowers*, vol. 2, 6.

39. Smith interprets the worm castings as an example of what he calls grotesque realism. See Smith, 248–52. See also Donald Ulin, "A Clerisy of Worms in Darwin's Inverted World," *Victorian Studies* 35, no. 3 (Spring 1992): 295–308.

40. Darwin, *The Formation of Vegetable Mould, through the Action of Worms, with Observations on Their Habits* (New York: D. Appleton & Co., 1897), 313.

41. Ibid., 313.

42. Smith, 246.

43. Darwin, *The Formation of Vegetable Mould*, 125

Evolution and Homogenic Love in C. R. Ashbee's Guild of Handicraft
Angelina Lucento

1. Edward Carpenter, *Homogenic Love and Its Place in a Free Society* (Manchester: Labour Press Society Limited, 1894).

2. Alan Crawford, *C. R. Ashbee: Architect, Designer, and Romantic Socialist* (New Haven: Yale University Press, 1985), 9–17.

3. See William Morris, *A Dream of John Ball* (Hammersmith: Kelmscott Press, 1892), and Stephen Eisenman, "Communism in Furs: A Dream of Prehistory in William Morris's *John Ball*," *Art Bulletin* 87, no. 1 (March 2005): 92–110.

4. Edward Carpenter, *Civilization: Its Cause and Cure and Other Essays* (New York: Humboldt Publishing Company, 1891), 44–58.

5. Gavin De Beer, "Biology before the *Beagle*," in *Darwin: A Norton Critical Edition,* 3rd ed., ed. Phillip Appleman (New York: W. W. Norton, 2001), 34–35.

6. Ibid., 34.

7. Ibid., 35.

8. Carpenter, *Civilization*, 52.

9. Ibid., 50–51.

10. Ibid., 52–53.

11. Ibid., 53.

12. Ibid., 53.

13. Edward Carpenter, *The Art of Creation* (London: George Allen & Unwin, 1921), 226.

14. Ruth Livesey, "Morris, Carpenter, Wilde, and the Political Aesthetics of Labor," *Victorian Literature and Culture* 32, 2 (2004): 610–11.

15. Carpenter, *Civilization*, 37.

16. Ibid., 37.

17. Ibid., 37–38.

18. Carpenter wrote in *Homogenic Love* that he preferred the term "homogenic" to "homosexual" because the latter, "generally used in scientific works, is of course a bastard word, i.e., from two roots, one Greek and one Latin. 'Homogenic' has been suggested, as being from two roots, both Greek, i.e., *homos* 'same,' and *genos* 'sex.'" See Carpenter, *Homogenic Love*, 4.

19. Ibid., 4.

20. Ibid., 15.

21. Ibid., 18, 48.

22. Carpenter was particularly keen on the works of the following scientists: the Berliner Albert Moll, the Viennese Richard von Krafft-Ebing, the Frenchman Paul Moreau, and the Italian Cesare Lombroso, among others; see Carpenter, *Homogenic Love,* 17–24. For his discussion of man's inherent tendency toward homogenic love and his argument for its necessity, see Carpenter, *Homogenic Love,* 27, 43–44.

23. Ibid., 44–45.

24. Ibid., 45.

25. Ibid., 48, 121.

26. Ibid., 48.

27. Excerpt from Ashbee's journal entry from September 5, 1886, quoted in Crawford, 23.

28. For a more detailed discussion of the university settlement movement, see Crawford, 24–28.

29. Ashbee's views on the role of machinery and mechanical reproduction are clearly delineated in his *An Endeavour Towards the Teaching of John Ruskin and William Morris* (London: Essex House Press, 1901), 19.

30. William Morris, *A Dream of John Ball*, in *William Morris: Poet, Artist, Socialist,* ed. Francis Watts Lee (New York: Humboldt Publishing, 1891), 23–117; Eisenman, 92.

31. James W. Hulse, *Revolutionists in London* (Oxford: Clarendon Press, 1970), 53; Pyotr Kropotkin, *Kropotkin: Selections from His Writings,* ed. Herbert Read (London: Freedom Press, 1942), 148.

32. Chushichi Tsuzuki, *Edward Carpenter, 1844–1929: Prophet of Human Fellowship* (Cambridge: Cambridge University Press, 1980), 92; Kropotkin, 148.

33. C. R. Ashbee, *An Endeavor Towards the Teaching of John Ruskin and William Morris,* 44–45. This philosophy—that if man's propensity toward communism is suppressed and not allowed to manifest itself in a productive manner, such as workers' guilds or trade unions, it will inevitably emerge in the form of revolt—seems remarkably similar to that expressed by Morris in *A Dream of John Ball*, with one exception: Morris's philosophy of the communist impulse lacked the homogenic component that Ashbee was so invested in. See Eisenman, 99.

34. Ashbee as quoted in Mary Greensted, *An Anthology of the Arts and Crafts Movement: Writings by Ashbee, Lethaby, Gimson, and Their Contemporaries* (Hampshire: Lund Humphries, 2005), 32. See also Ashbee, 19–25.

35. Richard Hofstadter, "The Vogue of Spencer," in *Darwin: A Norton Critical Edition*, ed Phillip Appleman (New York: W. W. Norton & Company, 2001), 392.

36. Crawford, 28.

37. Ibid., 34.

38. Ibid., 3.

39. Excerpt from an 1888 entry in Ashbee's journal, quoted in Crawford, 37.

40. Crawford, 37–39.

41. Ibid., 43.

42. Ashbee, 22.

43. Ibid., 24, 47.

44. Ibid., 47.
45. Ibid., 27.
46. Ibid., 29.
47. For an explanation of the silversmith's technique, see Crawford, 326–27.
48. Ibid., 327.
49. Ibid., 331.
50. Alan Crawford, Mary Greensted, and Fiona MacCarthy, "Furniture," in *C. R. Ashbee and the Guild of Handicraft* (Cheltenham: Cheltenham Art Gallery and Museum, 1981), n.p.
51. Ibid.
52. Ibid.
53. "The Guild of Handicraft: A Visit to Essex House," *The Studio* 11 (1897): 28–36; excerpts reprinted in Greensted, 30–31.
54. Crawford, 109.
55. Ibid., 126–27.
56. For Ashbee's opinion on the need for such educational initiatives, see Ashbee, 1–6.
57. Crawford, 145.
58. Ashbee, 29.

C. F. A. Voysey: An Aesthetic of Independence and Interdependence
Zirwat Chowdhury

1. Charles F. A. Voysey, *Individuality* (London: Nadder Books, 1986), 9. The text was originally published in 1915.
2. C. F. A. Voysey, "Quality of Fitness," *The Craftsman* (November 1912): 181.
3. Wendy Hitchmough, *C. F. A. Voysey* (London: Phaidon, 1995), 27.
4. Ibid., 30.
5. Voysey, *Individuality,* 14.
6. Reverend Charles Voysey, *Some Thoughts on Evolution: A Lecture in Reply to the Question: Are Any of the Operations of Law in Nature the Working Out of a Preconceived Plan?* (London: Williams and Norgate, 1888), 13.
7. Ibid., 6.
8. Ibid., 7–8.
9. Voysey, "Quality of Fitness," 181.
10. Stuart Durant, *The Decorative Designs of C. F. A. Voysey: From the Drawings Collection, The British Architectural Library, The Royal Institute of British Architects* (Cambridge: Lutterworth Press, 1990), 25.
11. Arthur Mackmurdo, *Pressing Questions: Profit-sharing, Women's Suffrage, Electoral Reform* (London: John Lane, 1916), vii.
12. Charles F. A. Voysey, *Reason as a Basis of Art* (London: Elkin Mathews, 1906. Pamphlet.), 20.
13. John Ruskin, quoted in Mackmurdo, *Pressing Questions,* 301.
14. Ibid., 305.
15. Ibid., 304.
16. C. F. A. Voysey, " Ideas in Things," in *The Arts Connected with Building: Lectures on Craftsmanship and Design delivered at Carpenters Hall Wall* (London: Batsford, 1909), 106.
17. Charles F. A. Voysey, "1874 and After," *Architectural Review* 70 (October 1931).
18. Chas. F. Annesley Voysey, "The Aims and Conditions of the Modern Decorator," *Journal of Decorative Art* 15 (1895): 88.
19. Ibid.
20. Voysey, "1874 and After."
21. Voysey, "Quality of Fitness," 174.
22. Voysey, "1874 and After."
23. Voysey, *Individuality,* 121.
24. Voysey, *Reason as a Basis of Art,* 7.
25. Voysey, "Ideas in Things," 101.
26. Ibid., 117.
27. Voysey, "1874 and After."
28. Voysey, *Individuality,* 12
29. Hitchmough, *C. F. A. Voysey,* 10–13. When Voysey was a young boy, Reverend Voysey was excommunicated for having challenged the divinity of Christ in a sermon. The result was the famous Healaugh trials, which not only led to the Reverend's exit from the Church of England but also to his foundation of the Theistic Church.
30. Ibid.
31. Voysey, "Ideas in Things," 64.
32. Voysey, "1874 and After."
33. Voysey, *Individuality,* 64.

PLATES

Following are reproductions
of selected works from the
exhibition *Design in the Age
of Darwin: From William Morris
to Frank Lloyd Wright*, grouped
by designer. The information
for each object has been
simplified to include designer,
title (if available), date,
workshop or manufacturer
if relevant to the design,
material, size, and collection.
Dimensions are given in
inches; height precedes width
precedes depth or diameter.

The Grammar of Ornament

3
CHRISTOPHER DRESSER
(British, 1834–1904)
Pitcher, ca. 1880
Linthorpe Art Pottery
Earthenware
9-1/4 x 5
Collection of Crab Tree Farm

4
CHRISTOPHER DRESSER
(British, 1834–1904)
Vase, ca. 1880
Linthorpe Art Pottery
Earthenware
8-1/2 x 5-1/2
Collection of Crab Tree Farm

5
CHRISTOPHER DRESSER
(British, 1834–1904)
Jar with Lid, ca. 1880
Linthorpe Art Pottery
Earthenware
6-1/2 x 7-1/2
Collection of Crab Tree Farm

6
CHRISTOPHER DRESSER
(British, 1834–1904)
Vase (also known as *Goat Vase*),
ca. 1893
Ault Pottery
Earthenware
10-1/4 x 7
Collection of Crab Tree Farm

7
CHRISTOPHER DRESSER
(British, 1834–1904)
Vase (also known as *Tongue Vase*),
ca. 1893
Ault Pottery
Earthenware
12-1/2 x 7
Collection of Crab Tree Farm

8
CHRISTOPHER DRESSER
(British, 1834–1904)
Vase, ca. 1880
James Couper & Sons
Glass
10 x 5
Collection of Crab Tree Farm

9
CHRISTOPHER DRESSER
(British, 1834–1904)
Pitcher, ca. 1895
James Couper & Sons
Glass
6-3/4 x 9-1/2
Collection of Crab Tree Farm

10
CHRISTOPHER DRESSER
(British, 1834–1904)
Teapot, 1880
James Dixon & Sons
Silver plate and ebony
9 x 5-1/2
Collection of Crab Tree Farm

11
CHRISTOPHER DRESSER
(British, 1834–1904)
Teapot and Creamer, 1880
James Dixon & Sons
Silver plate and ebony
5-1/4 x 8; 3-1/4 x 5
Collection of Crab Tree Farm

12
CHRISTOPHER DRESSER
(British, 1834–1904)
Tea Kettle, ca. 1880
Benham & Froud Ltd.
Copper and brass
8 x 5-1/2 x 5-1/2
Collection of Crab Tree Farm

13
CHRISTOPHER DRESSER
(British, 1834–1904)
Watering Can, ca. 1885
Benham & Froud Ltd.
Brass
22-1/2 x 13-1/2
Collection of Crab Tree Farm

14
CHRISTOPHER DRESSER
(British, 1834–1904)
Basket, 1881–82
Hukin & Heath
Silver and wicker
5 x 7-3/4
Victoria and Albert Museum,
London, Seawolf: 9-2004

15
CHRISTOPHER DRESSER
(British, 1834–1904)
Candle Holders, ca. 1883
Perry, Son & Co.
Silver plate and wood
5-1/4 x 5-1/2
Victoria and Albert Museum,
London, Seawolf 8:1/Seawolf
8:2-2004

16
CHRISTOPHER DRESSER
(British, 1834–1904)
Traveling Teaset, 1893–95
Hukin & Heath
Silver, wicker, and leather
3-1/4 (teapot)
Victoria and Albert Museum,
London, Seawolf 2:1-10

17
CHRISTOPHER DRESSER
(British, 1834–1904)
Soup Tureen, 1880–81
Hukin & Heath
Silver and ebony
7-1/4 x 12
Victoria and Albert Museum,
London, Seawolf 4:1-2004

18
CHRISTOPHER DRESSER
(British, 1834–1904)
Decanter, 1881
Hukin & Heath
Glass, silver plate, and ebony
8-1/4 x 5-1/2
Collection of Crab Tree Farm

19
MAY MORRIS
(British, 1862–1938)
Tablecloth, ca. 1890
Morris & Co.
Linen and silk
53 x 51-1/2
Collection of Crab Tree Farm

20
WILLIAM MORRIS
(British, 1834–1896)
Wandle, textile, 1884
Morris & Co.
Block-printed on cotton
45 x 37
Collection of Crab Tree Farm

21 (following page)
WILLIAM MORRIS
(British, 1834–1896)
Fruit (also *Pomegranate*),
wallpaper, 1866
Morris & Co.
Block-printed on paper
26 x 19-1/4
Collection of Crab Tree Farm

22 (following page)
WILLIAM MORRIS
(British, 1834–1896)
Willow Boughs, wallpaper, 1887
Morris & Co.
Block-printed on paper
26-1/2 x 21-3/4
Collection of Crab Tree Farm

23
C. F. A. VOYSEY
(British, 1857–1941)
Card Table, ca. 1900
J. S. Henry & Co.
Oak, copper, and felt
34-1/2 x 47 x 47
(with leaves extended)
Collection of Crab Tree Farm

24
C. F. A. VOYSEY
(British, 1857–1941)
*Side Chair with Double Heart
Motif*, ca. 1898
Oak and rush
52 x 16 x 16-1/4
Collection of Crab Tree Farm

25
C. F. A. VOYSEY
(British, 1857–1941)
Clock, ca. 1895
Wood, metal, and glass
21 x 10-1/2 x 7
Collection of Crab Tree Farm

26
C. F. A. VOYSEY
(British, 1857–1941)
Fireplace, ca. 1900
Cast iron
52-3/4 x 33-1/2 x 6-1/2
Collection of Crab Tree Farm

27
C. F. A. VOYSEY
(British, 1857–1941)
Donnemara Rug, ca. 1900
Wool
46 x 37
Collection of Crab Tree Farm

28
C. F. A. VOYSEY
(British, 1857–1941)
The River Mat, design, 1903
Watercolor on paper
21-1/4 x 10-1/2
Collection of Crab Tree Farm

29
C. F. A. VOYSEY
(British, 1857–1941)
Oswin, textile, 1896
Alexander Morton & Co.
Woven wool
85 x 60
Collection of Crab Tree Farm

30
C. F. A. VOYSEY
(British, 1857–1941)
Purple Bird, textile, 1898
Alexander Morton & Co.
Silk and wool double cloth
14-1/4 x 35-1/4
Collection of Crab Tree Farm

31
C. F. A. VOYSEY
(British, 1857–1941),
The Saladin, wallpaper, ca. 1897
Block-printed on paper
27-1/2 x 20-3/4
Victoria and Albert Museum,
London, Circ.261-1953

32
C. F. A. VOYSEY
(British, 1857–1941),
The Tokio, wallpaper, 1894
Machine-printed on paper
29 x 20-3/4
Victoria and Albert Museum,
London, Circ.267-1953

33
C. F. A. VOYSEY
(British, 1857–1941)
Bird in a Tree by Water's Edge,
design, 1893–96
Watercolor and pencil on paper
21-3/4 x 18-3/4
Victoria and Albert Museum,
London, E.146-1974

34
C. F. A. VOYSEY
(British, 1857–1941)
Seagulls, design, ca. 1890
Watercolor and pencil on paper
21-1/4 x 30-3/4
Victoria and Albert Museum,
London: Given by Courtaulds Ltd,
E.149-1974

35
C. F. A. VOYSEY
(British, 1857–1941)
Purple Bird, design, 1897–99
Watercolor and pencil on paper
24 x 20
Victoria and Albert Museum,
London: Given by Courtaulds Ltd,
E.176-1974 (T.136)

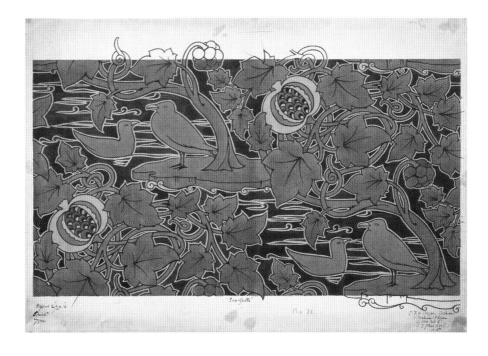

36
C. F. A. VOYSEY
(British, 1857–1941)
Bird, Fruit, Flowers, design, 1893
Watercolor and pencil on paper
26-1/2 x 17
Victoria and Albert Museum,
London, E.145-1974

37
C. F. A. VOYSEY
(British, 1857–1941)
Vine and Bird, design, 1899
Watercolor and pencil on paper
24 x 20
Victoria and Albert Museum,
London: Given by Courtaulds Ltd,
E.180-1974 (T.136)

38
C. F. A. VOYSEY
(British, 1857–1941)
*Design for Broadleys, Winder-
mere, for Mr. A. C. Briggs*, 1894
Watercolor and pencil on paper
30-3/4 x 21-3/4
Victoria and Albert Museum,
London: Presented by the Artist,
E.252-1913(V.1)

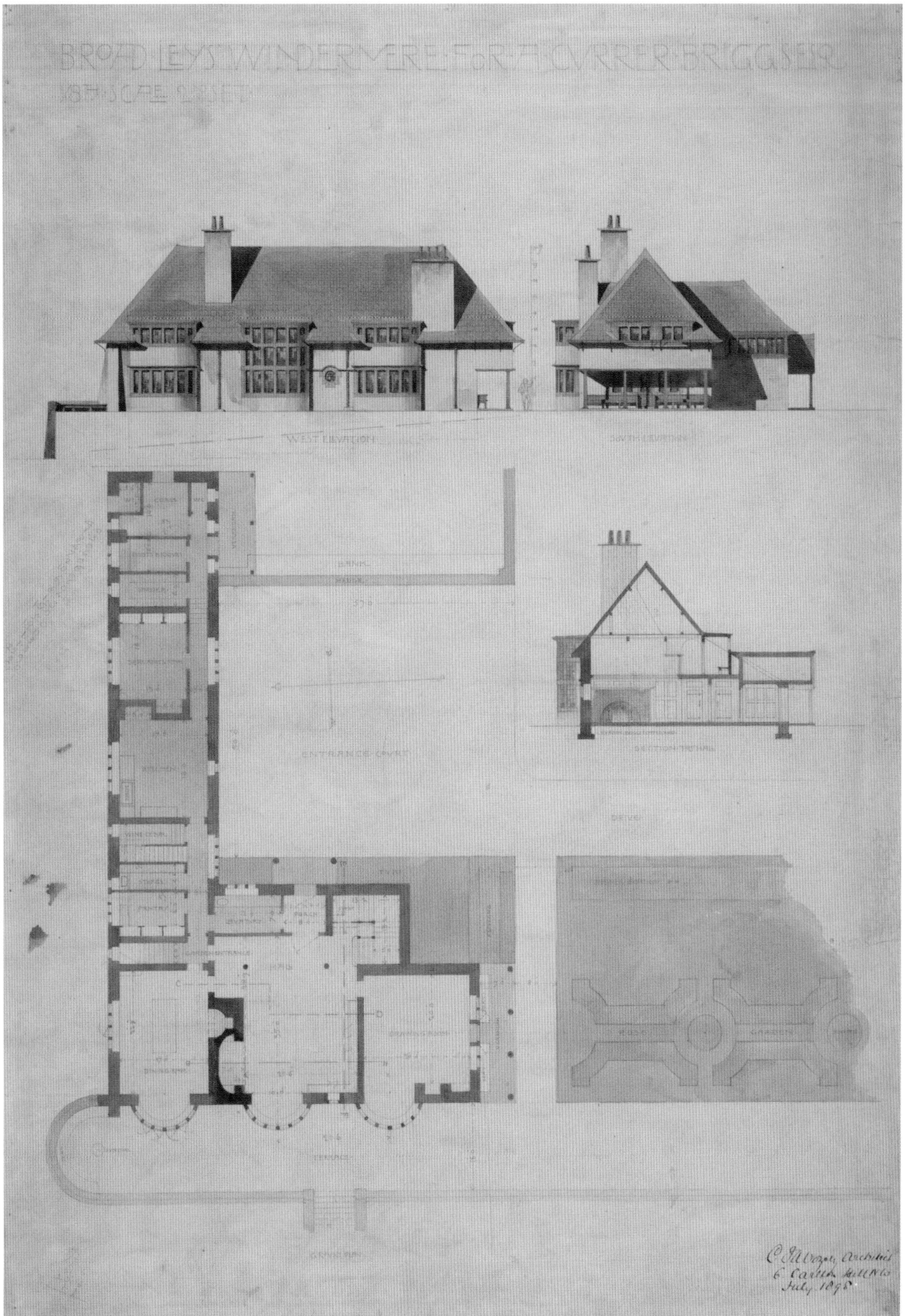

BROAD LEYS WINDERMERE FOR A CURRER BRIGGS ESQ

WEST ELEVATION

SOUTH ELEVATION

SECTION DETAIL

ENTRANCE COURT

C F A Voysey Architect
6 Carlton Hill NW
July 1898

39
C. R. ASHBEE
(British, 1863–1942)
Jar, ca. 1901
Guild of Handicraft
Glass, silver, and gemstone
7 X 5
Collection of Crab Tree Farm

40
C. R. Ashbee
(British, 1863–1942)
Salt Cellar, ca. 1901
Guild of Handicraft
Glass, silver, and gemstone
1-1/4 X 3
Collection of Crab Tree Farm

41
C. R. ASHBEE
(British, 1863–1942)
Salt Cellar, ca. 1901
Guild of Handicraft
Silver and gemstones
6-1/2 x 2 x 2-1/4
Victoria and Albert Museum,
London, Circ.58-1959

42
C. R. ASHBEE
(British, 1863–1942)
Chalice, ca. 1895
Guild of Handicraft, Ltd.
Gilded copper
5-1/4 x 4
Collection of Crab Tree Farm

43
C. R. ASHBEE
(British, 1863–1942)
Muffin Dish, ca. 1900
Guild of Handicraft
Silver and gemstone
4-3/4 x 9-1/4
Collection of Crab Tree Farm

44
C. R. ASHBEE
(British, 1863–1942)
*Dish with Double Loop
Handles*, ca. 1900–01
Guild of Handicraft
Silver, enamel, and gemstone
3-3/4 x 9-3/4
Collection of Crab Tree Farm

45
C. R. ASHBEE
(British, 1863–1942)
Soup Tureen and Ladle,
ca. 1901
Guild of Handicraft
Silver, ivory, and gemstones
15-1/4 x 10-1/2; 12-1/2
Collection of Crab Tree Farm

46
C. R. Ashbee
(British, 1863–1942)
Butter Knives and Serving Spoon,
ca. 1900
Guild of Handicraft
Silver and gemstones
6 x 1
Collection of Crab Tree Farm

47
C. R. Ashbee
(British, 1863–1942)
Cigarette Box, ca. 1904
Guild of Handicraft
Silver and enamel
2-1/2 x 4-1/2 x 3-3/4
Collection of Crab Tree Farm

48
Louis Sullivan
(American, 1856–1924)
Lunette, Scoville Building,
ca. 1885
Terra cotta
29 x 57-1/2 x 9
The University Museum,
Southern Illinois University
Edwardsville, 1974:0051

49
Louis Sullivan
(American, 1856–1924)
Chimney Panel, Rubel
Residence, ca. 1884
Terra cotta
22-1/4 x 21-3/4 x 9
The University Museum,
Southern Illinois University
Edwardsville, 1966:0030

52
LOUIS SULLIVAN
(American, 1856–1924)
Post and Capital (detail),
Rubel Residence, ca. 1884
Cherry wood
89 x 11-1/2 x 11-1/2
The University Museum,
Southern Illinois University
Edwardsville, 1966:0044

53
LOUIS SULLIVAN
(American, 1856–1924)
Elevator Frieze, Chicago Stock
Exchange Building, ca. 1894
Cast iron
66-1/2 x 18-1/2
Collection of John Vinci;
courtesy of Richard Nickel
Committee, Chicago.

54
LOUIS SULLIVAN
(American, 1856–1924)
T-Plate, Chicago Stock
Exchange Building, ca. 1894
Bronze
15 x 17
Collection of John Vinci;
courtesy of Richard Nickel
Committee, Chicago

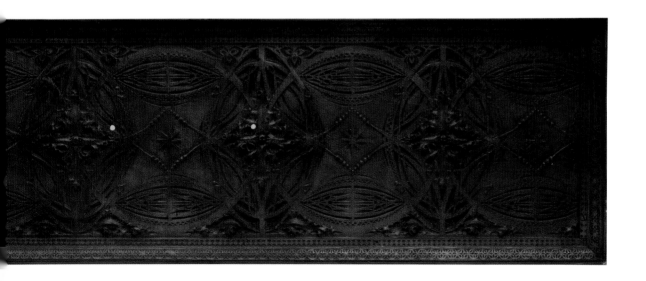

55
LOUIS SULLIVAN
(American, 1856–1924)
Elevator Door, Chicago Stock
Exchange Building, 1894
Bronze
83 x 28
Collection of John Vinci;
courtesy of Richard Nickel
Committee, Chicago.

56
LOUIS SULLIVAN
(American, 1856–1924)
Elevator Grille, Chicago Stock
Exchange Building, 1894
Cast iron
58-3/4 x 73-1/2
Collection of John Vinci;
courtesy of Richard Nickel
Committee, Chicago.

57
LOUIS SULLIVAN
(American, 1856–1924)
Doorknob and Plate,
Guaranty Building, 1895
Cast iron
14 x 4 x 4
The University Museum,
Southern Illinois University
Edwardsville, 1970: 0051

58
LOUIS SULLIVAN
(American, 1856–1924)
Doorknob and Plate,
Sullivan Residence, ca. 1892
Brass
11 x 3-1/2 x 3
The University Museum,
Southern Illinois University
Edwardsville, 1970: 0051

59
LOUIS SULLIVAN
(American, 1856–1924)
Baluster, Schlesinger & Mayer
(Carson Pirie Scott),
ca. 1898–99
Cast iron and copper plated
14 x 9-3/4 x 1
The University Museum,
Southern Illinois University
Edwardsville, 1966: 0146B

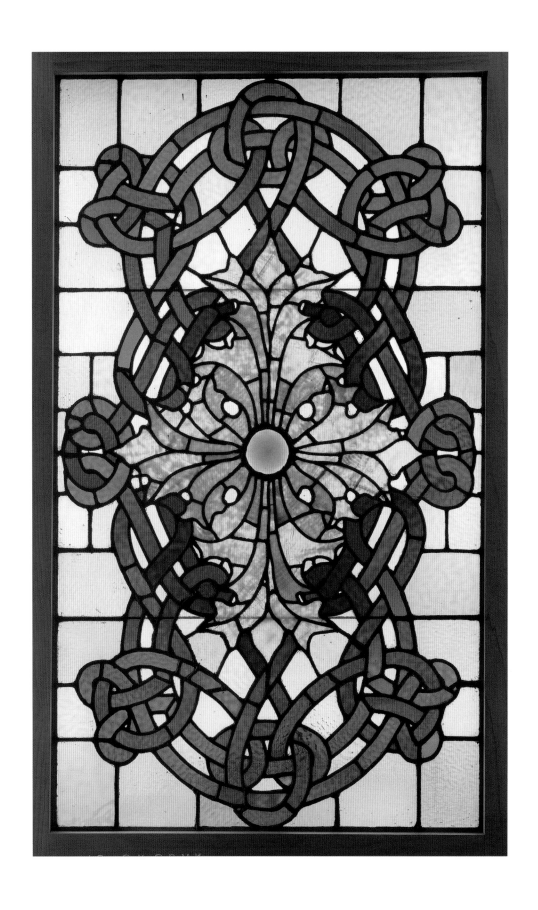

60
LOUIS SULLIVAN
(American, 1856–1924)
Window, Auditorium
Theatre, Chicago, 1889
Healy & Millet
Leaded glass and wood
56-1/4 x 33-3/4
Private collection

61
LOUIS SULLIVAN
(American, 1856–1924)
Design for Capitals,
Wineman Residence, 1882
Pencil on paper
25 x 28
Avery Architectural and
Fine Arts Library, Columbia
University in the City of
New York, 1965 001 00034

62
LOUIS SULLIVAN
(American, 1856–1924)
Design for Lunette,
Pueblo Grand Opera House,
ca. 1888
Pencil on tracing paper
21 x 19-3/4
Avery Architectural and
Fine Arts Library, Columbia
University in the City of
New York, 1965 001 00031

63
FRANK LLOYD WRIGHT
(American, 1867–1959)
Window, Frederick C. Robie
Residence, Chicago, ca. 1909
Wood and leaded glass with
metal hardware
48 x 38-5/8 x 3-1/2
The David and Alfred Smart
Museum of Art, The University
of Chicago; University Transfer,
1967.89

64 (below)
FRANK LLOYD WRIGHT
(American, 1867–1959)
Weed Holder, ca. 1890–1900
James A. Miller and Brothers
Copper
28-1/2 x 5
Frank Lloyd Wright Preservation
Trust, Gift of Dr. and
 Mrs. A. L. Burdick, 1996.01

65 (right)
FRANK LLOYD WRIGHT
(American, 1867–1959)
Urn, ca. 1900
James A. Miller and Brothers
Sheet copper
18-3/4 x 19-1/2
Victoria and Albert Museum,
London, M28-1992

66

67

68

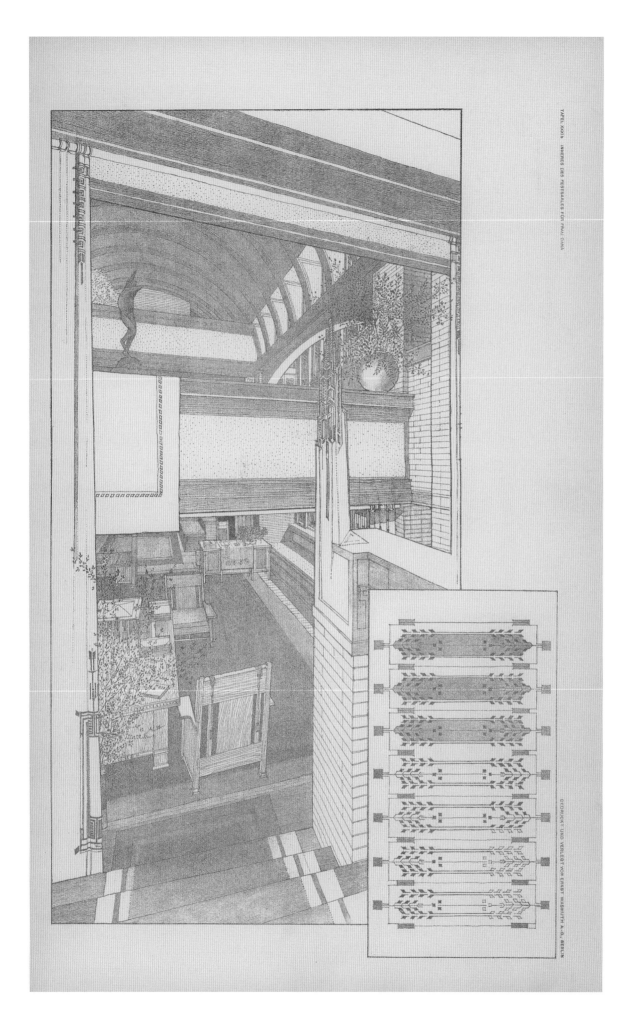

TAFEL XXXb INNERES DES FESTSAALES FÜR FRAU DANA

GEDRUCKT UND VERLEGT VON ERNST WASMUTH A.-G., BERLIN

69
FRANK LLOYD WRIGHT
(American, 1867–1959)
"Ballroom interior for
Mrs. Dana," from
Ausgeführte Bauten, 1911
Berlin: E. Wasmuth
25 x 16
Charles Deering McCormick
Library of Special Collections,
Northwestern University
Library

Photo Credits

Index